ISLAMIC FINANCIAL SERVICES IN THE UNITED KINGDOM

Edinburgh Guides to Islamic Finance
Series Editor: Rodney Wilson

A series of short guides to key areas in Islamic finance, offering an independent academic perspective and a critical treatment.

Product Development in Islamic Banks
Habib Ahmed

Islamic Financial Services in the United Kingdom
Elaine Housby

Islamic Asset Management
Natalie Schoon

Forthcoming
Shariah Compliant Private Equity and Islamic Venture Capital
Fara Ahmad Farid

ISLAMIC FINANCIAL SERVICES IN THE UNITED KINGDOM

Elaine Housby

Edinburgh University Press

© Elaine Housby, 2011

Edinburgh University Press Ltd
22 George Square, Edinburgh
www.euppublishing.com

Typeset in Minion Pro by
Servis Filmsetting Ltd, Stockport, Cheshire, and
printed and bound in Great Britain by
CPI Antony Rowe Ltd, Chippenham and Eastbourne

A CIP record for this book is available from the British Library
ISBN 978 0 7486 3997 7 (hardback)
ISBN 978 0 7486 3998 4 (paperback)

The right of Elaine Housby to be identified as author of this
work has been asserted in accordance with the Copyright,
Designs and Patents Act 1988.

CONTENTS

FOREWORD

This book describes Islamic financial services in the United Kingdom. It is the first book to look exclusively at this country. This is rather surprising when London is a major centre of the global Islamic finance industry. Perhaps, though, the very importance of the country internationally has obscured the situation of Muslims in the United Kingdom itself.

The book is an attempt to provide a comprehensive account of the Islamic financial services that are available in the United Kingdom at the present time. It is in the nature of such a study that aspects of it will quickly become outdated. This is particularly true of a study undertaken during a period of such upheaval in the world of finance. The book was begun at the time when a series of high profile bank failures were shocking the general public as well as the banking industry. On the one hand, this led to increased interest in the Islamic sector, which was perceived to have refrained from excessive risk taking, but, on the other hand, the commercial viability of Islamic services was also affected. Some products were withdrawn from the market during the period that this book was being written. Because this study seeks to present a complete history of Islamic finance in the United Kingdom, such recently discontinued products have still been described in detail. It is likely that some of them will reappear when the economic climate is more favourable.

A book published five years earlier would have presented a much more positive picture of unqualified growth and progress in the provision of Islamic financial services in the United Kingdom. It would not, though, have been any more accurate as a guide to future developments. There is no doubt that some of the early entrants to the market had unrealistic expectations of its potential. There seems to have been little serious research undertaken on what proportion of the British Muslim population might realistically be expected to prefer Islamic products. In some cases, even the estimate of the number of Muslims in the country that was used as a basis for calculation was exaggerated. At the time of writing there are signs of a backlash against these excessively optimistic growth forecasts, with Islamic finance in the United Kingdom being denounced as a failure. This is just as misguided. Simply failing to meet expectations that were always unreasonably high does not mean that Islamic finance in this country has been a failure. This study attempts to present a more balanced view of the sector's real strengths and weaknesses.

It is impossible to exclude completely all reference to the wider overseas market for financial services based in the United Kingdom. Most of them would not be viable if they were dependent on British Muslims alone, without the support of overseas customers and capital. This book, however, concentrates on activity within the country, since the international aspect has been written about elsewhere.

This is not primarily a theoretical work. The literature on Islamic economic thought is large, but only a small part of it looks seriously at the connection between theory and practice. To present the situation somewhat over-schematically, there are two types of people involved in the Islamic financial services industry: those who have trained in conventional finance and wish to add expertise in the Islamic sector to their skills, who usually wish to know only the basics needed to get a product passed as *shari'a* compliant;

and those who have studied the theory of Islamic economics, seek to transform the industry in the light of this and now find the practical reality falling painfully short of their ideals. The result is two types of literature on the subject which sometimes barely engage with each other. This book aspires to having something to say to both groups.

The terms United Kingdom and Britain have been used interchangeably throughout the book. This is not strictly speaking accurate, as the former term includes Northern Ireland and the latter does not. Nevertheless, the vast majority of the population of England, Scotland and Wales treat the terms as synonymous. Less excusably, the majority of the English population has a habit of treating both terms as synonymous with England. This book attempts to be scrupulous about which points apply to England and Wales (for legal purposes a single unit), which to Scotland and which to all three. Virtually none of the Islamic products described in this book are available in Northern Ireland.

The transliterations of the Arabic terminology of Islamic economics that are employed by banks and other participants in the field can vary noticeably. In direct quotations they have naturally been left in the original form, but the main text uses standardised spellings, where readability has sometimes been preferred to strict accuracy. Many of the scholars who endorse banks' Islamic services sign their names in Arabic script and subsequently feature in banks' literature in a variety of transliterations. A consistent version of their names has been used. Distinguished scholars of Islamic law are usually referred to with titles of respect such as 'sheikh' or 'mufti'. These have mostly been omitted, not with any intention to show a lack of respect, but because such titles are used inconsistently and convey little to the general reader.

Chapter 1 begins by giving a general account of the British

Muslim population and then outlines the essential principles of Islamic thought on financial matters. Chapter 2
relates the history of Islamic financial services in the United
Kingdom. Subsequent chapters deal in turn with each area
of financial services as they exist at present.

INTRODUCTION

The British Muslim population

Size and age profile of the population

The United Kingdom national census of 2001 was the first to include a question on the religious affiliation of respondents. This attracted a considerable amount of opposition from those committed to the view that the state should take no interest in such matters. Among communities of Muslim heritage, there were some who feared that the government's purpose in collecting such precise information on the location of Muslims was a sinister one. Despite this some Muslim organisations, notably the Muslim Council of Britain, campaigned vigorously for the inclusion of the religion question, in the belief that hard data on the Muslim population was a prerequisite for the provision of culturally specific services and the amelioration of discrimination and disadvantage.[1]

The census produced a figure of 1,591,000 Muslims in the United Kingdom, which is normally cited in the rounded form of 1.6 million. This appears to be reliable. Analysis of the data has shown that less than 1 per cent of respondents who gave their ethnic origin as South Asian took the option of declining to answer the question on religion (compared with over 7 per cent of the population as a whole). Despite the census figure being generally accepted as reliable, some Muslim organisations continued for some time after it became available to quote a higher figure, sometimes as high as 3 million, which was certainly not justified. The less inflated figure of 2 million has often been seen, perhaps simply because of the attraction of a round number, and it is probable that due to natural population increase the reality has by now caught up, and that this will be confirmed by the next census, which is due shortly after the publication of this book in 2011.

In the 2001 census Muslims formed 2.7 per cent, normally quoted in the rounded form of 3 per cent, of the British population. However, children of Muslim parents formed 5 per cent of the child population. The most significant aspect of British Muslim demographics is the youthfulness of the community. Around 60 per cent of British Muslims are under the age of 30. It is young adults who are the heaviest consumers of financial products and services, as they enter employment for the first time and make arrangements for the payment of their salary, buy a car and need to insure it, aspire to purchase their first home and eventually begin to make provision for their children's future and for their own retirement. The financial habits formed in early adulthood tend to be persistent and brand loyalty to banks is strong, so it is evident that a community with a high proportion of young adults in the present generation and the promise of even more in the next is particularly attractive to financial marketers.

Countries of origin

A large majority of British Muslims originate from the Indian sub-continent, that is, from Bangladesh, Pakistan and India. Based on census data, it is estimated that nearly three-quarters of British Muslims belong to families which migrated from these three countries. Of these, the largest group came from Pakistan. It would be fair to say that British Islam has a predominantly Pakistani character.

There are also sizeable communities of Turkish and Arab origin. Precise figures for these groups are not available because the ethnic categories used in the census did not give the option of identifying oneself as Arab or Turkish. It seems that many people of Arab or Turkish heritage ticked the box for 'White', while 'Arab' was the most common description written in by respondents who ticked 'Other'. The countries of the Arab world are, of course, very diverse politically and economically. Those who have come to the United Kingdom from the oil states have little in common with political refugees from Iraq or with the old established communities descended from Yemeni seafarers. Affluent citizens of the Gulf region have historically viewed the United Kingdom as a secure place to invest, a tendency which has been reinforced by the instability arising from the Iraq wars of 1991 and 2003. Arab Muslims have a much greater prominence in the sphere of Islamic finance in Britain than they do in British Islam generally, because of the fact that many Islamic financial products are targeted at least as much at wealthy expatriates, who may not hold British citizenship and may be resident in the country for only part of the year, as they are at British Muslims. This can give rise to certain tensions, which will be considered later in this book.

The population of Somali origin has grown over the last few decades as the political disintegration of Somalia continues. There are also small numbers of Muslims from other sub-Saharan African countries. African Muslims have to date been relatively neglected by researchers, and some believe that Somalis in particular are a largely hidden community. Since the 1990s a small number of Muslims have come to the United Kingdom from the successor states of the former Yugoslavia. In the last decade there has been a steady flow of refugees from Afghanistan.

It was the hope of some scholars of religion in modern Britain that the census would make possible a fairly precise estimate of the number of converts to Islam from other religious backgrounds. In England and Wales the inclusion of Arabs and Turks in the 'White' category made it impossible to distinguish, reliably, converts of European ethnicity, while 'Black' respondents might be Muslim by either birth or choice. In Scotland, the census included a different version of the enquiry into religion, which distinguished between religious affiliation at birth and religion at the present time and thus made conversion visible, but the numbers concerned were so small as to make meaningful extrapolation to the United Kingdom as a whole impossible. Anecdotally, it appears that some converts to Islam are prominent in Islamic activism in the United Kingdom, including the promotion of financial services.

Geographical location

There are large Muslim communities in West Yorkshire and Lancashire, in the city of Leeds and in towns such as Blackburn, Bradford, Dewsbury, Keighley and Oldham. Like the rest of the local population they have been left seriously disadvantaged by the decline of the local textile industry, an industry which originally enticed migrants from the Indian sub-continent to supply its labour requirements. These mill and factory workers mostly arrived through a process known as 'chain migration', in which early arrivals helped family and acquaintances back home to follow them. There is now a problem of a 'brain drain' of the most able and educationally successful Muslims from these declining northern towns to more prosperous areas, particularly London. The neighbouring city of Manchester has a substantial population of Pakistani origin, which developed as a result of a different migration pattern involving individual decisions by professionals to settle there, and these professional groups have been less affected by economic decline.

The city of Birmingham, England's second city, has a very large Muslim population, mostly Pakistani. Birmingham and Leicester, another city in the Midlands, are jointly predicted to become the first places in Britain where a majority of the population will be of non-European origin (a category which, of course, includes many groups other than Muslims). These cities are also notable for the degree of interaction between Muslim communities and the local academic institutions, and the amount of new thinking on Islamic matters which is generated there.

Naturally the capital city of London is home to large and diverse Muslim communities. The very diversity of the capital though means that no Muslim group has the amount of local influence possessed by those in Birmingham or Bradford. The Turkish population is almost entirely based in London and so are most of those of Arab origin, while about half of those of Bangladeshi origin are in London. The large and substantially impoverished Bangladeshi community in the borough of Tower Hamlets receives a considerable amount of media coverage due to its proximity to the centres of political and journalistic power. Luton, a city in the southeast close to London, has also attracted a lot of media attention to its large Muslim community.

In addition to the major areas of Muslim settlement described above, there are significant Muslim communities in most large English cities. In Scotland, nearly half of the Muslim population is in Glasgow and it is mostly of Pakistani origin. The Welsh capital Cardiff is home to

Bangladeshis, Somalis and Yemenis. There is also a small Muslim population in Northern Ireland.

Educational and occupational achievement

A major survey of ethnic minorities in Britain undertaken in 1994[2] found that Bangladeshis had the lowest achievement in school of any ethnic group, and that the second genera-tion had not improved much on the scholastic achievements of their parents. This situation, described then as 'extremely worrying', does not appear to have changed a decade later,[3] and this is probably the greatest cause for concern about the future of British Muslims. In contrast, Muslims from India are achieving better qualifications than the majority White students. Pakistanis rank below Whites, but above Bangladeshis, and unlike the latter do show improvement in the second generation.

Muslims of all origins have higher levels of participation in post-compulsory education than the majority popula-tion, and show strong commitment to the achievement of qualifications.[4] This commitment reflects an awareness that in a discriminatory labour market there is a need to have formal qualifications, and is linked to a preference for careers where clearly defined qualifications are the main recruitment criteria. However, the figures also show that on average Muslim students take longer to complete examina-tion courses, are more likely to achieve their qualifications at an older age and at university level attend less prestigious institutions.

Pakistanis and Bangladeshis have much higher rates of unemployment than the majority population, and it is especially concerning that the British-born generation has a higher percentage unemployed than its parents.[5] On the other hand, those of the British-born generation who are in work are tending to surpass the occupational level of their

parents. This contributes to a picture of economic polarisation among British Muslims. Because of a cultural preference that married women should not enter the labour
market, and a larger average family size than the general
population, the formal rate of unemployment probably
understates the extent of poverty among these communities.[6]

During the last forty years migrants of South Asian
origin, both Muslims and those of other religions, have
had a high level of self-employment. The Pakistani-owned
corner shop and the Bangladeshi-run curry restaurant have
been staple features of British life during this time. A study
of this phenomenon[7] found that typical shopkeepers were
not earning any more than they would as an employee, but
that they valued the independence and flexibility of self-
employment, the status they perceived it gave them within
the community and the opportunity for female relatives to
work in a culturally acceptable environment.

Interestingly, a large majority of the respondents in this
study did not want their children to take over their business, preferring them to enter a career that was less stressful
and better paid. The authors of the study argue that self-
employment may be only a transitory phase in the history
of immigrants' search for economic betterment, and that it
may propel the next generation into success in conventional
professions.[8]

Housing

Since the most important product now being offered
by the Islamic financial sector is home purchase finance,
it is relevant to consider the pattern of housing tenure
among British Muslims. In 2004 the Housing Corporation
(a government body concerned with the provision of social
housing) commissioned a detailed analysis of the data

from the 2001 census on Muslim housing circumstances, the first time this subject had ever been specifically studied. This report[9] found that 51 per cent of Muslims were home owners, compared with 69 per cent of the general population, and that while 18 per cent owned their home outright, 33 per cent were buying it with the help of some kind of bank loan. It was not possible to tell how many were using *shari'a* compliant bank finance. Of the rest of the Muslim population, 28 per cent lived in social housing, compared with 20 per cent generally, and 17 per cent were in privately rented accommodation, compared with 10 per cent generally. Muslim children were four times as likely as non-Muslim children to be living in overcrowded homes and twice as likely to be in a home without central heating (the absence of which in the British climate is regarded as an indicator of poverty).

These figures do not tell the whole story. There are considerable differences between Muslims of different countries of origin. The 1994 study mentioned above found that 45 per cent of Bangladeshis lived in social housing, while 79 per cent of Pakistanis owned their own home, a higher rate of owner-occupation than that found among the general population. This reflects the fact that migrants from Bangladesh arrived in the United Kingdom on average later than Pakistanis, after requirements to have lived in the local area for a certain length of time in order to qualify for council housing were lifted. Early migrants to the United Kingdom were not eligible for council housing and were often discriminated against in the private rental sector. They were thus pushed into buying houses if at all possible, and tended to end up in poor quality housing in disadvantaged areas. This pattern is still discernible, but is becoming less marked as subsequent generations find themselves unable to afford to buy their own home.

Religious leadership

The issue of imams who are perceived to be 'extremist' and out of touch with their British congregations has exercised politicians in the last few years, and has also received a considerable amount of media attention, much of it unhelpful. A recent serious study of the national and linguistic backgrounds of the imams of British mosques[10] tends to support the view that many of them are not well adapted to British life. It found that only 8 per cent were born in Britain and only 6 per cent stated that English was their first language (although many of the others spoke it as a second language). This is in contrast to the 48 per cent of the Muslim population they have come to serve who were born in Britain. Mosque committees, it seems, have a clear preference for recruiting from their country of origin rather than among religious scholars trained in Britain.

The author of this study observes that Urdu has become a marker of identity among British Muslims, so that even some respondents who might have been expected to see Bengali or Gujarati as their mother tongue claimed Urdu for this, and so did some of those born and educated in Britain. He also believes that Urdu is being 'sacralised' in the British context; that is, as it becomes increasingly remote as a language of everyday life, it is coming to be viewed primarily as a language of religious texts, in the same way as Arabic. The figures on the linguistic preferences of imams must, therefore, be considered with this in mind. It is also the case that most imams from overseas, once recruited, remain in place for many years.

Despite these provisos, there is reason to believe that those who are traditionally expected to provide religious leadership may be poorly equipped to offer guidance on the correct way for British Muslims to handle their financial affairs. A scholar who has received a conservative religious education in Pakistan may be inclined to take a rather simple view of *riba* and *gharar*, which may be unrealistic in the context of living, working and driving in modern Britain. In these circumstances, British Muslims, particularly younger ones, may seek out alternative sources of religious advice on these matters.

Many Muslims were proud that the census provided confirmation that they now formed the second largest religious community in the United Kingdom, after Christianity. At first sight the 3 per cent figure for Islam seems to trail a very poor second behind the 72 per cent for Christianity. These bald figures, however, obscure a more complex cultural reality. The proportion of nominal Christians who actually practice their faith actively is very low. While there are no hard figures on this, an estimate that 10 per cent of the population are regular church attenders has gained currency and seems plausible. Furthermore, Christianity in the United Kingdom is fragmented into a large number of church denominations which historically saw themselves as rivals. Some church leaders in fact expressed a preference for the inclusion in the census of separate denominations rather than a single 'Christian' category, but were overruled on this. Islam in the United Kingdom has been accommodated within a tradition of fissiparous Protestantism, rather than one of homogeneous Catholicism as in France, a difference that has more influence on the way that British Muslims pursue cultural and political goals than is sometimes realised.

Demand for Islamic financial services

This brings us to the rather basic question of whether British Muslims are committed to the observance of Islamic precepts on financial matters. There is a recurrent assumption in writing on Islamic finance that all those of Muslim heritage actively desire *shari'a* compliant products. Sometimes this is due to sheer laziness of thought, sometimes there is a disingenuous marketing purpose behind it. There are remarkably few serious studies of demand for Islamic financial products among British Muslims. Welcome rectification of this omission looks likely to come from work by postgraduate students over the next few years, but in the meantime a lot of guesswork is involved.

Some firm evidence is provided by a relatively small study,[11] which was cited in National Savings and Investments' survey of the prospects for Islamic products[12] in the apparent absence of any other readily obtainable research into these issues. This study of around 500 Muslims in several British cities found that only about a quarter cared strongly that their financial services should be *shari'a* compliant. Tellingly, it concluded that it would be necessary to increase this proportion by active marketing before an Islamic sector could thrive in Britain. It also found that desire for Islamic financial services was strongest among the more highly educated and more affluent respondents. If this finding is reliable it would be good news for providers. It may though simply reflect the fact that higher earners consume more financial services of all kinds, rather than that they seek out Islamic alternatives more actively, and one should also sound a note of caution about the possibility of respondents wishing to appear religiously observant to the interviewer.

An apparently contrasting conclusion emerged from the major study of ethnic minority Britons undertaken in 1994, which included sophisticated measures of cultural identity. It found that South Asians who adhered most strongly to the language, religion and culture of their country of origin were more likely to be living in poverty than those who presented a more 'assimilated' identity.[13] (The authors rightly caution against simple assumptions about the direction of causation here; poverty and unemployment make engagement with the majority language and culture much more difficult.) This finding would suggest that those with the greatest loyalty to Islamic teaching on financial matters were those of the least interest to the providers of financial services. The date of this study is now a generation ago, and it may be that it is the children of these respondents who are now driving the development of Islamic financial services, because they have achieved a level of income that makes it possible for them to exert more pressure on the banks than their parents could.

The study of self-employed South Asians undertaken in the 1990s found that 75 per cent of the Pakistanis interviewed (mostly first generation migrants) believed that their religion had a view on lending and borrowing money, but only 28 per cent of them said that religious considerations had influenced their own borrowing decisions.[14] The discrepancy was not due solely to religious indifference, but was also partly because they chose for other reasons to avoid commercial lenders. Compared with those of Indian and African-Asian origin in the study, the Pakistanis made more use of loans from family members and from government agencies and less of loans from banks and mortgages. There were indications that they were less likely than other ethnic groups to be approved for commercial loans, and in this we see an early indication of the complex interaction between the 'pull' factors of loyalty to cultural and religious traditions and the 'push' effects of economic disadvantage and discrimination by members of the majority population.

Principles of Islamic economic thought

It has been noted that over 1,400 of the 6,226 verses of the Quran refer to economic issues. The figure at once dispels the idea that economics is a peripheral or minor part of the religion of Islam. Given that much of the Quran was revealed in the context of the Prophet's attempts to establish and administer a religiously based city-state, it is natural that questions of correct economic behaviour were prominent in the minds of the believers. It is important to remember that Islam does not share the distaste for commerce that has been a prominent feature of the Christian tradition. In the harsh physical environment of the Arabian peninsula, where all natural resources were scarce, trade was a necessity for survival and the Prophet himself was a successful merchant. The Quran and Sunna are deeply marked by a trading culture, and the Islamic financial tradition shows a strong preference for structuring transactions as sale contracts.[15]

Of course, there are certain items in which it is absolutely forbidden to trade. These are, most straightforwardly, pork products and all alcoholic drinks. Contracts concerning the supply of these goods are treated by *shari'a* as legally unenforceable. Also forbidden are products and services connected with gambling or commodified sexuality. Some scholars regard music as *haraam* and some *shari'a* advisers prohibit investment in any aspect of the entertainment industry.

Gambling

The prohibition of gambling is based on a Quranic reference to the name of a particular game of chance popular in pre-Islamic Arabia, *maysir*. The consensus interpretation of this passage is that it intends to condemn all games of chance and related forms of gambling. (The fact that the English word 'hazard' is derived, via the French, from the Arabic word for dice, *zahr*, gives some indication of how popular gaming was in Arabia.) The passage which condemns *maysir* continues: 'By means of intoxicants and games of chance Satan wants only to sow enmity and hatred among you, and hinder you from the remembrance of God, and from prayer' (5:90–1). Note that the emphasis is on the tendency of both intoxicants and gambling to cause quarrels and aggression. This is a recurrent theme in the *fiqh* (Islamic legal) tradition on financial matters. Decisions on whether to permit or to disallow particular practices often seem to have been based on the likelihood of disagreements developing between the parties to the transaction.

In the modern world the development of forms of trading on the stock market which can appear to be no more than elaborate forms of gambling has opened up a new field of debate. The appearance of state-sponsored lotteries also represents a formidable form of *maysir*, and some Muslim community organisations in Britain have been confronted with the dilemma of whether to accept grants from public funds whose source is the National Lottery.

Uncertainty

There is some overlap between the prohibition of gambling and that of *gharar*, usually translated as 'uncertainty' or 'speculation'. The English language literature sometimes refers to 'aleatory contracts', by which is meant those whose outcomes are largely dependent on chance factors over which neither party to the transaction has any control. *Gharar* has not received the same attention as the much more widely known ban on interest, but it is a very important element of the Islamic tradition of commercial law.

The classical examples of contracts disallowed because of uncertainty are the sale of an unborn camel, independently of the mother, and of the fruit of an orchard before it is ripe. A related prohibition is that of the sale of goods not under the seller's control. The classical example of this was a runaway animal, but the paradigmatic modern example is a stolen car. All sales where the price is not unambiguously stated at the time of agreeing the deal are outlawed. Any such expression as 'at the current market price' when this is not known to the purchaser is unacceptable, as is any commitment to purchase goods in the future at a price which cannot be known in the present. The argument is complicated by the fact that the Prophet is reported to have engaged in a sale with advance payment for future delivery, and since his behaviour is normative this has always been treated as a lawful form of sale, called *bay' salam*.

The scope of application of the principle of *gharar* has been enormously increased in recent times by the explosion in the world's financial markets. Despite the great flexibility and subtlety of the *fiqh* instrument of *qiyas* (analogy), a collection of precedents based on camels and date palms can be made to yield principles that can be applied to the fantastically complicated financial products currently on offer only with considerable difficulty. Even the apparently straightforward question of whether or not an item is under the seller's control can be very difficult to answer definitively. To date, Muslim thinkers have nearly always found trading in futures – that is, agreeing to buy goods for delivery at a future date with no certain knowledge of what the market price will be at that date – unacceptable as a clear example of *gharar*. This rules out a large proportion of the activity on modern financial markets. However, Islamic thought in this area is developing very rapidly. While everyone agrees that speculation is forbidden, product developers are often reluctant to concede that their own bright idea constitutes speculation.

Insurance

The main reason for being uncomfortable with insurance is that it appears to fall under the prohibition of uncertainty in contracts, because there is no way of knowing whether the client will ever need to claim, or what relation any payment made may bear to the amount paid in premiums. It has been felt that if the customer successfully makes a large claim after paying only a small amount in premiums he or she has effectively got something for nothing, which falls under general disapprobation in Islamic thought. On the other hand, if the customer never needs to make a claim, the insurance company is getting something for nothing. The counter-argument is that the premiums are in no way related to placing bets on future events, they are payments made for the provision of a service, in the normal manner. The service provided by the insurer is to guarantee security and peace of mind to the client, and this is accomplished quite independently of whether or not the client ever needs to make a claim.

Life insurance is particularly problematic for most Muslim writers. It has never entirely been freed from a sense that it entails trying to know the mind of God, that speculating on the date of one's death is somehow blasphemous. The obligation to take out life insurance to provide security for a mortgage provider constitutes an additional reason for mortgages being problematic for some Muslims. The counter-argument is that ensuring provision for one's dependants after one's death is a religious duty and what any loving and responsible head of household should do. To emphasise this aspect, Islamic providers normally refer to life insurance as 'family' insurance or *takaful* (the *shari'a* compliant form of insurance).

Interest payments

The most characteristic feature of Islamic banking, and the aspect of this subject best known to non-Muslims, is the avoidance of paying or taking interest. The sources from which this principle is derived are, in fact, complex and disputed. In brief, modern bank interest is identified with *riba*, which is condemned on several occasions in the Quran. This word comes from a root which means to grow or increase. The clearest and most widely quoted Quranic condemnation of it is: 'devour not *riba*, doubled and re-doubled' (3:130). Most commentators consider that this refers to a pre-Islamic practice of those who might in modern parlance be described as 'loan sharks', whereby a debtor unable to repay his loan on the due date would have the period allowed for repayment doubled in exchange for a corresponding doubling of the debt. Such an obvious example of the exploitation of the poor by those richer and more powerful evidently aroused the anger of the Prophet. This practice is referred to as *riba al-jahiliyya* (the *jahiliyya* being the pre-Islamic period). Some legal commentators have taken the view that it is this specific form of extortionate interest only that is outlawed, but they are very much in a minority. The consensus has always been that all forms of 'increase' on loans are outlawed. The only kind of loan (*qard*) permitted is a *qard hasan*, or 'good loan', which is an interest-free loan given essentially as an act of philanthropy to those in distress, with no possibility of compelling repayment. The principle of the *qard hasan* is now being invoked in some commercial contexts.

The other main source for the law on *riba* is this *hadith*, which exists in several slightly different versions:

> Exchange gold for gold, silver for silver, wheat for wheat, barley for barley, dates for dates, salt for salt, measure for measure and hand-to-hand. If the exchanged articles belong to different genera, the exchange is without restraint provided it takes place in a hand-to-hand transaction.[16]

From this was developed the theory of two types of ille-gitimate gain: *riba al-fadl* (increase through excess, or, in other words, not 'measure for measure') and *riba al-nasi'a* (increase through delay, in other words, not 'hand-to-hand').

The four major schools of law (Hanafi, Hanbali, Maliki and Shafi'i) developed numerous differences in the way they identified the *'illa* (efficient cause) of the instances men-tioned and applied *qiyas* (analogy) to them to obtain prin-ciples that could be applied to other types of transaction. These differences still have some significance in modern times, and Islamic scholars in contemporary Britain cer-tainly still consider them. A large majority of British Muslims originate from South Asia where the Hanafi school prevailed and so this school is dominant in British Muslim legal thinking, while the global influence of Saudi Arabia has considerably increased the importance of the Hanbali tradition, historically the most geographically limited of the four schools. It would though be true to say that most of the younger generation of British Muslims, with whom this study is primarily concerned, have very limited knowledge of the *fiqh* tradition and do not concern themselves with the finer points of disagreement between schools.

Regardless of whether or not it is justified by the sources in Quran and Sunna, the identification of *riba* with bank interest is unshakeably fixed in the minds of the vast major-ity of Muslims, an identification reinforced by the English translation of the source material. In most cases the straight-forward view is taken that any kind of interest payment is *haraam*, without regard to the question of whether the value of the capital has actually increased. This issue has become pertinent over the last two years while interest rates have been negative, that is, they have fallen to a level below the rate of inflation, so that the real value of the capital has not been increased by them. Historically, it has been the opinion of at least some scholars that interest payments which do not increase the real value of the capital may be lawfully accepted by Muslims. The situation has also produced the parallel phenomenon of non-Muslims eschewing 'hoarding' in an Islamically approved manner, because leaving cash in an interest-bearing account has not generated any real profit.

One of the Five Pillars of Islam is the obligation to pay *zakat*. This can be described as a form of compulsory charity, but in practice it functions as a wealth tax. It is normally fixed at 2.5 per cent (the slightly cumbersome modernised form of the traditional one-fortieth) of all savings held for over a year by those whose wealth has passed a threshold known as the *nisab*, an amount traditionally expressed as a certain quantity of gold and silver. Some Islamic banks deduct *zakat* from their customers' accounts. The combined effect of the prohibition of *riba* and the enforcement of *zakat* is to produce a strong disincentive to leave money in a savings account for long periods. This habit is usually referred to disparagingly by enthusiasts for Islamic economics as 'hoarding'. The term deliberately echoes the language normally used for the selfish stockpiling of essential consumer goods at a time of shortage. The point repeatedly stressed by all writers on the subject is that money should circulate around society. It must be used for productive investment, not allowed to idle in an individual's bank account. More importantly, it must be constantly redistributed from the rich to the poor. The essential tendency of the system is to reduce inequality. There is a verse of the Quran which says this explicitly: 'let it [money] not just make a circuit of the wealthy among you' (59:7).

The debate on dar al-harb

Traditionally, all countries where Muslims are a minority have been treated as *dar al-harb*, lands of war, as opposed to the *dar al-Islam*. At least one legal school, the Hanafi, maintained that it was not necessary to observe injunctions such as the prohibition of *riba* when living outside the *dar al-Islam*, and that countries where Muslims were a minority continued to be *dar al-harb*. There has, therefore, been an incentive for Muslims who wished to engage in interest-based transactions with a clear conscience to continue to regard the countries to which they have migrated as *dar al-harb*. Some scholars still take this view, but it is becoming very difficult to sustain. The term *dar al-harb* implies that these countries have an actively hostile relationship with Islam, which most Muslims do not consider to be the case. (Although the Iraq war of 2003 has led to a reassessment of the question in some circles.) For those of the second generation who accept that the countries in which they were born are their real home and have no comforting 'myth of return', it is no longer possible to postpone the living of an observant Muslim life until they are living in a Muslim-majority country. The problems raised by attempts to make *halaal* products available to Muslim minorities in Europe are quite different from those involved in attempts to Islamicise a whole country, which was the preoccupation of the first generation of writers on Islamic finance.

The most celebrated recent example of the opinion that it is permissible for Muslims living in Europe to take out interest-based loans is the so-called 'Qaradawi *fatwa*'; that is, the opinion issued in 1999 by the European Council for Fatwa and Research, whose president was Yusuf al-Qaradawi. The *fatwa* was issued on the grounds of *darura*, necessity, and the lesser form of need, *haja*, taking account of the unsatisfactory nature of the housing available to large numbers of European Muslims, and the damage this was doing to the perpetuation of the Islamic faith in Europe, bearing in mind that the home is the prime locus of transmission of faith.[17] This *fatwa* shocked the burgeoning Islamic home finance industry in Britain, which saw that widespread reliance on it would be a threat to its market. These fears do not, however, seem to have been borne out.

Notes

1. This chapter draws heavily on the work of Serena Hussain in analysing the results of the 2001 census as they relate to Muslims. Hussain, Serena (2008), *Muslims on the Map: A National Survey of Social Trends in Britain*, London: Tauris.

2. Modood, Tariq and Berthoud, Richard (1997), *Ethnic Minorities in Britain: Diversity and Disadvantage*, London: Policy Studies Institute, p. 65.

3. Hussain, *Muslims on the Map*, p. 51.

4. Modood and Berthoud, *Ethnic Minorities in Britain*, p. 7.

5. Hussain, *Muslims on the Map*, p. 134.

6. Modood and Berthoud, *Ethnic Minorities in Britain*, p. 161.

7. Metcalf, Hilary, Modood, Tariq and Virdee, Satnam (1996), *Asian Self-employment: The Interaction of Culture and Economics in England*, London: Policy Studies Institute.

8. Metcalf *et al.*, *Asian Self-employment*, p. 121.

9. Sellick, Patricia, *Muslim Housing Experiences*, Housing Corporation, September 2004. This report can still be downloaded from www.housingcorp.gov.uk, even though the Housing Corporation has now been closed down, or it can be obtained from the Oxford Centre for Islamic Studies, who undertook the research for it.

10. Geaves, Ron (2008), 'Drawing on the past to transform the present: contemporary challenges for training and preparing British imams', *Journal of Muslim Minority Affairs* 28:1, 99–112.

11. Dar, Humayon A. 'Demand for Islamic financial services in the UK: chasing a mirage?', Loughborough University

Institutional Repository, 2004, available at: www.lboro.ac.uk/library.

12. *National Savings and Investments (NS&I) Sharia'a Compliant Investments Review*, September 2008, p. 8, available at: www.nsandi.com.

13. Modood and Berthoud, *Ethnic Minorities in Britain*, p. 164.

14. Metcalf *et al.*, *Asian Self-employment*, pp. 57–8.

15. Saleh, Nabil A. (1986). *Unlawful Gain and Legitimate Profit in Islamic Law*, Cambridge: Cambridge University Press, p. 34.

16. Nabil, *Unlawful Gain and Legitimate Profit in Islamic Law*, p. 34.

17. The justifications for this opinion are considered in detail in Caeiro, Alexandre (2004), 'The social construction of sharia: bank interest, home purchase and Islamic norms in the West', *Die Welt des Islams* 44: 351–37.

CHAPTER 2

HISTORY OF ISLAMIC FINANCIAL SERVICES IN THE UNITED KINGDOM

The first generation

It is important to bear in mind that a perceived need for complex Islamic financial products and services is not in any sense a traditional problem, but one that has been created by the demands of a modern economy. The majority of first generation Muslim immigrants to Britain came from rural areas with very little in the way of formal banking, Islamic or otherwise. The country to which they came, although much more highly developed than Pakistan or Bangladesh, had not yet entered the world of instant international money transfer and round-the-clock globalised stockmarkets in which we live today. In the 1950s and early 1960s, the period of peak immigration, most working-class people were paid in cash, credit cards had not been invented, loans and overdrafts were only available in exceptional circumstances, houses could sometimes be bought without borrowing and investing in the stockmarket was a specialised pastime of the affluent. There was just far less opportunity for questions of *riba* and *gharar* to arise.

I make this point to emphasise the fact that the Islamic financial services industry has not developed simply as part of an increased Muslim cultural assertiveness, but because the needs that it supplies have become far more pressing.

Some writing on Islamic finance in the United Kingdom seems to imply that it is a tradition which has been transmitted unchanged from a village in Pakistan to Canary Wharf, and this is simply not historically possible. This is not, of course, to deny the unchanging nature and eternal validity of the precepts of Islam in the eyes of believers, merely to point out that religious precepts are articulated in particular social and economic circumstances.

Several studies[1] of first generation migrants to Britain have described the popular institution of a savings club or *kameti*. For example, a group of ten men (at that time migrants were nearly all single men) each earning £20 per week could, by living in over-crowded rented houses, save half that sum and thus in ten weeks save £1,000 between them, a sum which could, fifty years ago, buy a terraced house in a working-class area. A house would be bought for the first member of the club, who would normally rent out rooms to others, and the whole group would continue to save in this way until everyone owned a house. The existence of this form of pooled savings helps to explain why families of Pakistani origin in Britain still have higher rates of property ownership than that of the general population. As mentioned in the previous chapter, early migrants were not eligible for council (social) housing and often faced discrimination from white landlords in the private rental sector. This forced them to rely on renting within their own community and striving to purchase property. Unfortunately, the need to own outright as soon as possible meant that the houses purchased were usually the cheapest and least desirable. An additional reason for wanting to purchase was that the house could be sold again on return to Pakistan to provide funds for setting up in business there. Since in the majority of cases this return never happened, a long-term pattern of residential concentration in disadvantaged areas was created.

The successful functioning of such savings clubs clearly required a very high level of mutual trust, which was facilitated both by the process of 'chain' migration and by a sense that only fellow countrymen could be relied on in a hostile wider society. As immigrants became better accepted by and integrated into the host society, the close bonds among the first arrivals which made such self-help schemes possible tended to be weakened. The emergence in modern times of financial services which explicitly invoke a Muslim community in the abstract could be seen in one sense as an attempt to recreate artificially the close kinship and friendship networks which sustained the first Muslim migrants.

There is some indication that the first generation's experience of housing insecurity has left a legacy of a strong desire for home ownership among those of migrant origin. There is also a marked cultural preference for home ownership among Britons as a whole. The percentage of owner-occupiers in the United Kingdom is much higher than in some other European countries. It is easy to see why the combination has made the United Kingdom the most fruitful country in Europe for the development of Islamic home purchase finance.

The first Islamic bank in Britain

The development of formal Islamic banking in the United Kingdom was probably delayed by the unfortunate history of the Bank of Credit and Commerce International (BCCI), which, although not in fact Islamic in its operations, was Muslim-owned and had targeted British Muslims as customers. Its messy collapse in 1991 amid allegations of large-scale fraud seems to have left the British regulatory authorities rather nervous of any bank explicitly aimed at the Muslim market.

The first true Islamic bank in Britain was Al Baraka,

founded in 1982 by the Al Baraka Investment Company, based in Jeddah, Saudi Arabia, and essentially a private company owned by Sheikh Saleh Abdullah Kamel, a wealthy Saudi who owned a number of small banks in various countries. It offered a range of banking services, including a form of Islamic home purchase finance, the first ever in the United Kingdom. Al Baraka claimed to have made a profit of £3 million in its last year of business. Despite this, the Bank of England was always unhappy about the fact that the bank was owned by a single individual, a situation which it was obliged to oppose in accordance with new regulations brought in after the collapse of BCCI. The fact that the stability of the bank depended entirely on the continued solvency and commitment of the sheikh was felt to expose account holders to an unacceptable degree of risk. An additional concern was that although the owner was based in Saudi Arabia the bank itself was not incorporated in that country and therefore not subject to any oversight in his home territory. The Bank of England allowed Al Baraka some time to seek diversification of ownership, but the problem could not be solved to its satisfaction. Some reports stated that the sheikh was reluctant to dilute his ownership and others that it was difficult to interest investors in an Islamic bank. The bank therefore decided to surrender its licence to offer banking services. It finally closed as a bank at the end of June 1993, though it continued to operate as an investment company.

A question was asked in the House of Commons on 28 April 1993 by Keith Vaz about the closure of Al Baraka Bank. Mr Vaz was a Labour Member of Parliament for Leicester, a city with a large community of South Asian origin, and was himself one of the first MPs of South Asian ethnicity. At the same time he asked questions about the closure of the Roxburghe Bank and Mount Bank, two banks recently closed down by the regulators due to insolvency, which although not Islamic had served the South Asian community in particular, and whose disappearance had left this community feeling the absence of banking staff who could speak community languages. In his written reply to Mr Vaz the Chancellor confirmed that after extensive discussions with the Bank of England about its ownership structure Al Baraka Bank had decided to discontinue its deposit facilities and repay all depositors. The reply also made it clear that 'the intended surrender of the bank's authorisation had arisen as a result of the new Basle supervisory requirements and not as a result of financial deficiency or its existence as an Islamic bank'. Despite these reassurances, the fact that the bank was closed down even though it was apparently profitable caused resentment among some British Muslims and a lingering suspicion that the regulators were applying stricter standards to an Islamic bank than to conventional ones. The authorities have been trying to dispel such suspicions ever since.

A notable feature of the story of the closure of Al Baraka was the loyalty shown to the bank by its customers, some of whom had expressed interest in a plan to sell shares in the bank to its account holders. Rather than rushing to withdraw funds when closure was threatened, in a manner which has become all too familiar to conventional banks in recent years, customers and supporters stood by Al Baraka and in some cases made offers of financial assistance. Indeed, staff had to be employed to return deposits to account holders who had ignored requests to remove their funds.[2]

The historical significance of Al Baraka was that it made the first clear statement in the United Kingdom about the existence of a unique tradition of economic thinking within Islam, and the need and desire of Muslims for financial services which respected that tradition. For most non-Muslims this was the first time that the concept of Islamic banking had been brought to their attention. There was then still little sense in the wider society of Muslims as a distinct community. It was usual to refer to 'Asians', meaning those with family origins in the Indian sub-continent, without distinction of religion. The then governor of the Bank of England, Edward George, was quoted in the wake of the closure of Al Baraka as saying that he could see no need for a special bank catering for the Asian community and hoped that existing banks could meet their needs.[3] It will be seen that awareness of Islam among bankers subsequently increased considerably and that Mr George himself became a important figure in the development of Islamic finance in the United Kingdom.

A new Islamic home purchase plan

The next major development in the availability of Islamic financial products in the United Kingdom was the introduction of home purchase finance by the United Bank of Kuwait in 1997. The bank had introduced a specialist Islamic division to its UK operation in 1991. This was eventually named the Islamic Investment Banking Unit, the name under which it still operates. The United Bank of Kuwait later merged with the Al Ahli Bank and is now known as the Al Ahli United Bank.

The house purchase product was given the brand name of Manzil, which means 'dwelling'. The introduction of this service released considerable pent-up demand. The manager responsible has described how it took his department several weeks to process the enquiries generated by one brief television report.[4] Initially, Manzil offered only a *murabaha* product, but in 1999 it introduced an *ijara* version. The latter has proved far more popular. These products are discussed in detail in Chapter 5. Briefly, under a *murabaha* contract the bank buys the property and resells it to the customer at a higher price, while under an *ijara* contract the bank buys the property and the customer purchases the equity in instalments while paying rent for the use of the share still owned by the bank.

Although Manzil finance was available to all, in practice there were several factors which made it difficult for the ordinary British Muslim to take advantage of its new availability. Under the Manzil scheme the bank was prepared to lend only 80 per cent of the valuation of the property, so the purchaser required a 20 per cent deposit. This was difficult for many people on average earnings to save up, and compared unfavourably with the very high loan to valuation ratios then frequently offered by conventional mortgage providers. In addition, the monthly repayments were higher than with a conventional mortgage. For these reasons it attracted mainly higher earners and affluent Arabs wishing to invest in UK property.

The ordinary British Muslim also needed to make a conscious effort to contact Manzil as he or she was unlikely to come across it by chance. The bank had branches only in London, and had no high street presence until 2005 when it reached agreement with the West Bromwich Building Society to distribute its Islamic home purchase plans. The West Bromwich had a large branch network and was based in the West Midlands, the location of some of the largest Muslim residential concentration in the United Kingdom. By that time Manzil had competition from other Islamic providers.

Islamic finance on the high street
In July 2003, HSBC, the giant international bank, introduced an Islamic current account and Islamic home purchase finance in the United Kingdom (though the home

purchase plan was available only in England and Wales). The bank's Islamic division is called Amanah, meaning 'trust', in both the everyday and the technical financial sense. It had built up considerable experience in the Muslim majority world, and so the establishment of Amanah UK was a logical next step. HSBC has at least one branch in virtually every town of a reasonable size in the United Kingdom, and is thus an everyday presence to British Muslims in a way that the Arab banks were not. Specialist Amanah counters were set up in branches with a significant Muslim population locally and prominent posters displayed in the windows of such branches. Enquiries about Amanah products could though be made through any branch of the bank. The HSBC Islamic home finance service thus had true mass market availability. It also attracted the attention of the media in a way that Islamic finance never really had before. Several widely read newspapers appeared intrigued by the possibility of a bank making a profit without charging interest. Many of the general public became aware of Islam's ban on interest for the first time as a result of the HSBC publicity campaign.

HSBC originally offered an *ijara* contract, but has now switched to a diminishing *musharaka* scheme. In this latter model, the bank and the client are joint owners of the property, with the client buying out the bank's share of the equity in instalments and paying rent for the use of the proportion of the property still owned by the bank. The main difference from an *ijara* model is that the client is described as a joint owner from the outset rather than as a tenant until all payments have been completed. There were some legal issues raised by the client being technically a tenant under an *ijara* contract until completion of all the payments. This situation had worried the Council of Mortgage Lenders during the government initiated consultation process, as they feared that with an *ijara* product the bank could become liable for landlord's responsibilities such as repairs to the property, and were concerned that in case of default by the purchaser the bank would have to seek eviction under English tenancy law rather than repossession under the law relating to a mortgage charge over the property.

The first independent Islamic bank

The Islamic Bank of Britain (IBB) was authorised by the Financial Services Authority (FSA) in August 2004. It represented another major step forward, because it was the first stand-alone Islamic bank, a company offering a full range of banking services in *shari'a* compliant form. The particular attraction of its self-contained structure is that its Islamic services are not cross-subsidised by a large conventional banking operation, as with banks that have only an Islamic 'window', and thus appear to many Muslims to be more strictly *halaal*. There is a direct relationship between money coming in and money going out, and because of this the IBB did not introduce home finance until 2008, as it initially needed to concentrate on attracting deposits. The first branch was opened in September 2004 in Edgware Road, London, the centre of an area of Arab residential concentration which already contained a large number of businesses catering for Arab and Muslim customers. The administrative headquarters of the bank are in Birmingham, where there is a large Muslim workforce available, but rents and salaries are lower than in London.

The initial start-up capital of the bank was subscribed by a group of investors in the Gulf who had a knowledge of and interest in the United Kingdom and believed that a bank dedicated to the needs of the British Muslim market could be very successful. In October 2004, it was launched on the London Stock Exchange and has been able to raise additional capital by issuing shares. A large proportion of its shares are still owned by members of the al-Thani family of Qatar and by commercial interests in the same country. During the first few years of its operation the IBB made heavy losses, but allowance had been made for this. Its growth has been slowed by the recession and by the requirement for increased capital reserves imposed by regulators, but it has done better than some cynical commentators expected. Although it has not yet moved into profit, it has reduced its operating losses and continued to expand its branch network, its range of services and its customer base. At the time of writing it has a total of eight branches: four in London, two in Birmingham, one in Leicester and one in Manchester. Its products and services will be considered in detail in the relevant chapters.

Competition on the high street

Lloyds TSB bank entered the Islamic market in February 2005 when it began to offer an Islamic current account and Islamic home purchase finance through branches with a large number of local Muslim potential customers. Lloyds, like HSBC, was a ubiquitous high street presence and could easily reach the ordinary British Muslim. Its entry into the market signified that there was now a real, diverse Islamic financial services sector in the United Kingdom, within which British Muslims could choose on the basis of price and convenience, just as in all other aspects of their lives as consumers, rather than being limited to the choice between one Islamic product and all of the non-*shari'a* compliant ones.

The particular home finance product offered by Lloyds TSB was called Al-buraq and was actually a product of the Arab Banking Corporation (ABC), based in Bahrain. The ABC made an agreement in 2005 for its Islamic home finance to be marketed in the United Kingdom through Bristol & West, a former building society which was by then a division of the Bank of Ireland, and it was Bristol & West who supplied Al-buraq home finance to Lloyds. Unfortunately, this arrangement has been a victim of the much more cautious mood currently prevailing in the banking industry. The Bank of Ireland decided that it wished to reduce its mortgage business in the United Kingdom generally, and it ceased accepting new customers for Al-buraq home finance in May 2009. It continues to service previously existing contracts. At the time of writing Lloyds are looking for an alternative partner to enable the bank to resume offering Islamic home finance.

The situation in Scotland

Ahli and HSBC home finance plans are available only for the purchase of properties in England and Wales. This is not a point given much emphasis in their publicity, and habitual English chauvinism has resulted in HSBC, in particular, being regularly described in the media as offering Islamic home finance in 'the UK'. The Muslim population of Scotland is a very small proportion of the total Muslim population of the United Kingdom, and it does not include any of the wealthy overseas visitors who feature prominently in the calculations of banks. The IBB, showing that it takes its name seriously, will also advance finance for the purchase of properties in Scotland.

The other bank which includes Scotland in its home finance plan is the United National Bank (UNB), which introduced a *shari'a* compliant home finance product designed for the Scottish legal system in 2004, beating the IBB to this by five years. The UNB is a division of a Pakistani bank and caters particularly for the British population of Pakistani origin. It claims that all of its staff are bilingual in English and Urdu. This is in contrast to the Arab links of many of the other Islamic providers and supplies a need keenly felt by older British Pakistanis and those who are frequently visited by members of their extended family in the sub-continent. The inclusion of Scotland in the UNB's provision is probably due to the presence of a sizeable community of Pakistani origin in Glasgow, where it has a branch. The UNB is not a purely Islamic bank, but offers both conventional and Islamic services, which presents a challenge to the common assumption that all British Muslims naturally prefer Islamic services if they are available. The UNB claims to have been 'the first bank to offer Islamic mortgages in the UK market', but since it was only registered in the United Kingdom under its present name in 2001, having been formed from a 'joint venture' of the National Bank of Pakistan and United Bank Limited of Pakistan, and Ahli offered 'Islamic mortgages' in 1997, this claim does not appear to be accurate, unless it is intended to mean that UNB was the first bank to offer Islamic home finance throughout the whole of the United Kingdom.

Prior to the banking crisis of 2007–8, some other British banks, notably Halifax Bank of Scotland (HBOS) and the Royal Bank of Scotland, had expressed interest in entering the Islamic market. This would have increased competition and thus brought down prices, and would also have led to Scotland being better served. In the event HBOS was taken over by Lloyds TSB at the urging of the British government, a merger which has reduced competition even in the conventional banking industry in the United Kingdom to a worrying extent. The Royal Bank of Scotland, meanwhile, is now majority-owned by the government and is struggling to recover from huge losses. It is very unlikely to be entering any adventurous new markets in the near future.

Taxation and regulation

The first Islamic home purchase plans were disadvantaged by the British property taxation regime then prevailing. Stamp duty land tax is payable on completion of the purchase of all property over a certain value. It consists of a percentage of the purchase price and the percentage itself increases in higher price bands. In a *murabaha* contract legal title to the property is transferred twice, when the bank buys it and when it resells it to the client, and this triggered two charges of stamp duty. Because the resale price is higher, the second stamp duty charge would be higher and in some cases could take the price into a valuation band where a higher percentage of the purchase price was charged. The same problem arose under an *ijara* contract when title was transferred to the client after completion of the instalment payments.

This liability to double stamp duty on *murabaha* contracts was removed by the British government in 2003, and on *ijara* and *musharaka* contracts in 2005. This reform is thought to have stimulated the market to offer more *shari'a* compliant home finance. It was the first major change made in response to a study of the legal and fiscal obstacles to the development of the Islamic financial services sector in the United Kingdom undertaken by a working party set up in 2001. This group comprised representatives of the Treasury (the finance department of the British government), the Financial Services Authority, the Council of Mortgage Lenders, several banks and some Muslim organisations, and also some individual experts on the subject. It was set up by Edward George, then governor of the Bank of England, after consultation with Gordon Brown, the Chancellor of the Exchequer (finance minister), and was chaired by Andrew Buxton, a former chairman of Barclays Bank and director of the Bank of England.

A problem with Islamic home finance plans that has proved to be more difficult to resolve is that they cannot be used by tenants of social rented housing to purchase their home on favourable terms under the so-called 'right to buy' scheme. This is because the provisions of the scheme stipulate that only the present occupier can buy the property and that it cannot be resold for a specified number of years without heavy financial penalties. These provisions are intended to prevent the scheme being misused to make a profit by buying houses at the discounted price offered and reselling them quickly at the full market value. Unfortunately, these stipulations also prevent the use of *ijara* and *murabaha* contracts, because they involve a third party in the sale. This worries the government, because one of the main reasons for encouraging the development of Islamic financial services was to promote access to the housing market among disadvantaged Muslim communities. The problem particularly affects those of Bangladeshi origin, a very high proportion of whom occupy council or housing association homes (although, since this community is also on average the most impoverished Muslim group, it is likely that many of them would be refused finance by banks in any case), and it seems likely that a special exemption for Islamic contracts under the 'right to buy' scheme will eventually be introduced.

A continuing source of concern and some resentment to the Islamic sector has been the regulations concerning required capital reserves. This has been a recurrent theme from the days of Al Baraka onwards. The percentage of its liabilities that a bank is required to hold in reserve varies according to the assessed riskiness of each type of debt. Historically, Islamic products have been considered to be higher risk than conventional ones, mainly due to a lack of data on their long-term performance, and this has restricted the activities of Islamic banks. For example, when it first introduced home finance Ahli Bank was not able to offer as many home loans against the same amount of capital as a conventional mortgage provider, because Islamic home purchase plans were assessed as being twice as risky as conventional ones and therefore requiring twice as much capital.

The literature on Islamic banking over the last twenty years is full of references to the regulations on capital adequacy produced by the Basle Committee on Banking Supervision, versions 1 and 2, and of discussion on how these could be made fairer to Islamic providers. The banking crisis of 2007–8 has led to a complete reassessment of the capital adequacy regulations for all banks and it is too early to say how the new requirements will impact on Islamic banks. It seems likely though that the favourable impression made by the greater stability of the Islamic sector during the crisis (leaving aside the problems with *sukuk*) will help to secure more sympathetic treatment in the future.

Legal issues

Historically, the English legal system has been the favoured jurisdiction for Islamic contracts, even when the parties are based abroad. This is partly due to the perception that English common law based on precedent is a better fit with the Islamic legal tradition than the codified legal systems of most of continental Europe, and partly to the long colonial history of British involvement with the Arab world and the Indian sub-continent. This provides an interesting example of a fruitful exchange of ideas developing out of political and economic relations which were originally essentially exploitative. The question of how precisely *shari'a* fits into English law is a delicate one. The English secular courts have been quite clear that they cannot and should not adjudicate on questions of religious principle.

The case of *Shamil Bank of Bahrain* v. *Beximco Pharmaceuticals (and others)*, decided in January 2004, is considered to be a key test case in this regard. The parties to the dispute stipulated that their original agreement should be governed by English law, even though none were based in England, and included a clause to this effect in the contract. When the bank pursued the company over its failure to repay funds advanced to it, the English high court had to judge the case. Beximco argued that the contract actually stated that 'subject to the principles of the Glorious Sharia'a, this agreement shall be governed by and construed in accordance with the laws of England', and that therefore *shari'a* took precedence. In an attempt to avoid repaying the money, it claimed that the original agreement was *haraam* and that therefore it could not be compelled to honour it. (The funds were, in fact, advanced to them under *murabaha* contracts, so any decision that these were unacceptable in *shari'a* would have caused a great many problems in the wider world of Islamic finance.) The ensuing legal debate established three principles: that having agreed that the contract was acceptable in Islam at the time they signed it, the defendants could not change their opinion of the religious principles involved to suit themselves at a later date; that *shari'a* was not a formal code of law that could be interpreted by a secular court; and that, even if had been, since a contract could not be governed by two legal jurisdictions simultaneously the law of England must be the only one which applied.

More recently another case has aroused concern that English courts may be retreating from the position that they cannot get involved in questions of religious principle. The Investment Dar of Kuwait attempted to avoid repayment of a debt to Blom Bank of Lebanon by arguing that the contract was void as it was not *shari'a* compliant. In

December 2009 an English judge, while ruling that the debt should be repaid, commented that Investment Dar at least had 'an arguable case'. This alarmed many people working in Islamic financial services, since if taken seriously such a view would render all Islamic contracts unreliable. It seems though very unlikely that an English court would ever refuse to enforce a lawfully made contract because of differing interpretations of religious compliance.

The active encouragement of the Islamic financial sector in the United Kingdom by public agencies has aroused anxiety in some quarters that Islamic religious principles are being surreptitiously incorporated into the country's legal system, but this is largely due to a misunderstanding of the nature of so-called Islamic law. Specific legal issues will be considered in appropriate chapters.

Islamic savings and investments

Throughout the last twenty years Islamic investment funds have continued to multiply, with mixed fortunes. This is by far the easiest area of financial services to enter with a product marketed specifically as Islamic, since the only difference from conventional investment is that the companies whose stocks are traded must be religiously acceptable. The ease of launching an Islamic fund and the temptation of high net worth Muslims with large amounts of money to invest in the United Kingdom has led to a rapid turnover in the sector, with a number of funds appearing, performing poorly and disappearing again, although, of course, there have been some which have done well. Not only the financial performance of Islamic funds is unpredictable, there is also considerable scope for disagreement and error in the screening of companies for *shari'a* compliance. In this respect the immense advances in computer software and global communications in recent years have been a central factor in the development of this area. It is now much easier to obtain information about companies and to analyse them for compliance in sophisticated ways.

The lack of savings accounts which do not pay interest has been a problem for British Muslims for decades. Some of them have resorted to requesting their bank to withhold the interest due on their account or to donating the interest to charity. In the last few years though a number of Islamic savings accounts have appeared. Because an Islamic deposit account cannot pay a formally fixed rate of return, *shari'a* compliant savings accounts are actually profit-and-loss-sharing accounts. The money is invested and a share of the profit paid to the account holder. The usual practice is to 'smooth' the returns paid so that they are predictable, regardless of the ups and downs of the investment performance. As with home purchase finance, the development of such accounts was initially hindered by unfavourable tax treatment, as profit-and-loss-sharing accounts were treated as equity investments rather than cash deposits and, therefore, potentially subject to additional taxes. In 2005 this situation was amended as part of the continuing efforts by the Treasury to make tax treatment of Islamic finance more equitable.

Corporate Islamic banking

The last five years have seen rapid developments on the wholesale and corporate side of Islamic banking. The European Islamic Investment Bank was incorporated in the United Kingdom in January 2005 and approved by the FSA in March 2006, opening for business the following month. This was the first stand-alone Islamic investment bank in the United Kingdom. The Bank of London and the Middle East was incorporated in August 2006 and approved by the FSA in July 2007. It is also an entirely Islamic bank, offering *shari'a* compliant investment and financing for companies and high net worth individuals. Gatehouse Bank was established in May 2007 and approved by the FSA in August 2008. It is an entirely *shari'a* compliant wholesale investment bank. All these banks sought to bring together the financial expertise available in London, increasingly regarded as a global centre of Islamic financial services, with the wealth and the investment opportunities available in the Muslim-majority world. The concerns of the ordinary British Muslim did not feature prominently in their statements of purpose. The rapid growth of the Islamic sector does though offer worthwhile employment opportunities for British Muslims.

Academic activity

One of the first institutions to pursue active theoretical research into Islamic banking was the Islamic Economics unit of the Islamic Foundation, based in Markfield near Leicester. During the 1980s and 1990s this unit did important work in translating and making available books about Islamic economics first published abroad, particularly in Pakistan, during a period when there was little original work appearing in English on the subject. For some years in the 2000s it collaborated with Loughborough University in the provision of a postgraduate degree course in Islamic banking and economics. This has now been discontinued, but the Markfield Institute of Higher Education continues to teach some courses on the subject. In recent years a number of other British universities and business schools have begun to offer courses on Islamic banking and economics, both as modules on general finance or business courses and in the form of self-contained Masters degrees. They continue to see an increase in the number of students interested in studying the subject, despite, or perhaps because of, the crisis in the banking industry.

The future

The previous Labour government was committed to encouraging Islamic finance. It is too early to say whether the new coalition government will continue its policies in this area, but there is no obvious reason why it should not. In 2006 Gordon Brown, then still Chancellor, confirmed to a conference which took the phrase as its title that he wanted London to be 'the gateway to Islamic finance and trade'.[5] In December 2008 the Treasury produced a report[6] on the Islamic financial sector, a general survey of activity and problems in the industry with suggestions on what could be done to help. The government made it clear that its aim was, in that overworked phrase, 'a level playing field'. It said repeatedly that it was not seeking to promote the Islamic sector above the conventional one, or to give Islamic providers any especially favourable treatment, but merely to ensure equality of treatment. The distinction is a fine one when achieving this level playing field requires so much government activity. Some critics might say that making any changes at all, for example, to liability for stamp duty land tax, in itself constitutes special treatment.

The Treasury has been thinking about issuing *sukuk* since at least November 2007 when it issued a consultation paper on the topic, and the prospect of a UK government *sukuk* issue caused considerable excitement in the world of Islamic finance. At the time of writing, however, there are still no firm plans in this regard. The delay has been due partly to the economic recession and partly to the legislative issues raised. The story is told in detail in a later chapter.

Other countries aspire to challenge the position of the United Kingdom as the leading centre of Islamic financial services in the non-Muslim world. Just across the Channel,

President Sarkozy of France is seeking to build up the financial services industry in Paris until it becomes a serious rival to London. Developing an Islamic sector is an important element of a financial industry that aspires to be truly global, and the large French Muslim population (about twice the size of the British one) would provide a strong domestic base for Islamic services. So far though moves in this direction have come up against the French tradition of state secularism, which makes it difficult to introduce any legal or fiscal changes to accommodate Islamic financial models. The British tradition has been to demonstrate the religious neutrality of the state by treating all religions equally rather than by refusing officially to acknowledge any of them, and to date there has been no serious political opposition to the changes made to accommodate Islamic financial products. The financial services industry in Australia is also keen to develop an Islamic sector with global reach, and is well placed to do so, combining as it does its English language and legal heritage with proximity to Malaysia (a world leader in Islamic finance), and being in a time zone which makes its office hours complementary to those of London. The United Kingdom, however, has built up a real depth of expertise in Islamic finance and is never likely to be entirely displaced as a global centre of the industry. In future it may have to work harder to retain talent, as there continues to be an international shortage of staff qualified in the unusual combination of skills needed for Islamic banking and these skills are highly portable. London is more likely to be able to prevent its key industry personnel from being lured to countries with better weather if they are people whose roots are in the country of which it is the capital. The real challenge now facing the Islamic financial services industry is to ensure that its benefits are shared by the British Muslim population as a whole.

Notes

1. See particularly Shaw, Alison (1988), *A Pakistani Community in Britain*, Oxford: Blackwell, pp. 42–3. Shaw's informants told her that the most common reason for not taking out a conventional mortgage was simple ignorance of their availability, rather than religious objections.
2. The events behind the closure of Al Baraka are summarised in *British Muslims Monthly Survey*, April 1993 and *Q News*, 2–9 July 1993.
3. Quoted in *British Muslims Monthly Survey*, January 1994. Mr George was speaking in an interview with the magazine *Garavi Gujarat*.
4. Leach, Keith, 'Islamic home finance in the UK: structures, Barnes and market experience', *New Horizon*, June 2003.
5. Brown, Gordon, 'Britain – the gateway to Islamic finance and trade', *New Horizon*, July–August 2006.
6. HM Treasury (2008), *The Development of Islamic Finance in the UK: The Government's Perspective*, available at: www.hm-treasury.gov.uk.

CHAPTER 3

PERSONAL ACCOUNTS

Current accounts

In the past it was usual for current (cheque) accounts in the United Kingdom to pay no interest and to charge transaction fees. This was the product of a banking culture in which most people chose a bank as a teenager when they first began work or university and stayed with it for the rest of their lives, and worried more about whether their bank manager was satisfied with their own conduct of their account than about whether the bank was delivering good service to the customer. About twenty-five years ago, in the wake of the liberalisation of banking regulation undertaken by the Conservative government of the period, banks began to behave more like any other provider of consumer goods and services and to encourage customers to move their account to whichever one was offering the best deal. As part of this new competition for customers they began to pay interest on current accounts. This, of course, made them less attractive to devout Muslims, not more. The interest paid is always a very low rate, far lower than the rate of interest paid on savings accounts, but to most Muslims it is the principle of *riba* which matters, not the rate.

Those customers determined to avoid receiving interest

eventually ran out of accounts to move to as non-interest paying current accounts disappeared from the mass market. After this there was the choice of accepting the money and paying it to charity or requesting the bank to withhold the interest. A 1999 survey[1] of banks' policies on dealing with the refusal of interest by customers showed a confused picture, with some banks saying they gave it to charity, some that they kept it and some that legally they were not allowed to keep it. As a rule banks find it difficult to comply with a request not to pay interest on an individual account, even if staff are sympathetic, because their computer systems are set up to add interest to all accounts automatically and the cost of altering this for one customer is far greater than the amount of the interest saved. In any case, some Muslims feel that letting a bank keep the interest it would otherwise have paid merely allows it to invest more in its *haraam* activities. Even donating the interest to charity is not straightforward, as some Muslim charities will not mix donations of interest money with their general funds, regarding it as tainted money whose use can be justified only in emergency relief situations.

Another aspect of the intense competition between banks is that overdraft facilities have become generally available on current accounts, rather than having to be granted as a special favour. Typically today a customer who has a regular salary paid in to the account can be £500 overdrawn without previous arrangement. Of course, banks charge a high rate of interest even on such authorised overdrafts, and they also deduct punitive charges from the accounts of customers who are more in debt than they are authorised to be. Now that they have been obliged to drop fees for routine transactions, banks make very little profit from an account which is never in debt, and the resulting ambiguity of the banks' position, being dependent on the interest and fees charged for a form of borrowing which they profess to deplore, has been blamed by some for helping to create the credit bubble which burst in 2008.

So a demand was created in the Islamic sector of the market for an everyday cheque account that neither paid nor charged interest. Of course, it was also necessary for the funds in these accounts to be held and invested only in a religiously acceptable manner. In the case of the conventional banks with Islamic windows, such accounts appeared at the same time as the introduction of Islamic home purchase finance, and were probably to some extent subsidised by the profits made on the latter. Current accounts have not been threatened by the recession, as have other kinds of Islamic products, since there is no risk to the bank involved.

HSBC

HSBC Amanah UK, the bank's Islamic division, offers a *shari'a* compliant current account.[2] This account was introduced at the same time as the Amanah home finance plan in July 2003, and was the first Islamic current account to be available in the United Kingdom. It offers the usual current account facilities of cheque book, debit card, standing orders and direct debits. There is no overdraft facility and no credit interest is paid, so the account is free of *riba* either paid or received. Because the money deposited in the account makes no return of any kind, there is no problem about the safety of the funds and their return on demand being guaranteed. The fees charged on this account are in line with those charged for the bank's conventional current account, that is, everyday transactions are free but special services and purchases overseas incur fees.

The close integration of the Islamic 'window' into the bank as a whole has both advantages and disadvantages. On the one hand, the fact that HSBC is a household name and has branches everywhere in the country means that it is easily accessible to any British Muslim. Customers who did not previously know that an Islamic account was available may come across the details in the bank's general information material and perhaps decide to open an Islamic account rather than a conventional one. The fact that Amanah has a giant multinational bank behind it means that it can offer competitive terms and avoid charging the sort of fees that a stand-alone Islamic bank may have to. Some British Muslims were very grateful to HSBC for making a *shari'a* compliant current account available to them for the first time.

On the other hand, this very degree of integration with the conventional banking world is a negative factor for some Muslims. The bank's account information assures the enquirer that money in an Amanah account is 'kept separate from conventional funds and not used to generate interest', but there is some public scepticism about the extent and effectiveness of this separation. Some potential customers feel that Amanah is effectively underwritten by the bank's conventional business and thus in a sense not contributing fully towards the development of a truly independent Islamic finance industry. There is no real feeling of separation in either the experience of walking through an HSBC branch to reach the Amanah counter at the back, or that of clicking on links in Amanah's website only to find oneself back at a page of information intended for conventional accounts.

The *shari'a* advisers of Amanah UK are those on the bank's central international committee, which does not contain any British representation. It presently consists of Nizam Yaquby, Muhammad Elgari and Imran Usmani. The information booklet about the current account, unlike that for the bank's home purchase plan, does not mention the names of these scholars at all.

Islamic Bank of Britain

The Islamic Bank of Britain (IBB) also offers a current account with all the usual facilities that people expect from a conventional current account, that is, a cheque book, a debit card and the facility to make direct payments into and out of the account.[3] As with all the IBB's accounts, the bank promises that the customer's money will not be invested in *haraam* products. Those specifically mentioned are alcohol, pork and pornography.

The customer's money is described as a loan to the bank, a *qard hasan* or non-profit-making loan. Naturally, the money paid in does not earn any credit interest. Because the money does not increase in any way, it can be guaranteed. The bank states that 'obviously it has to be paid back to you, in full, on demand'.

Cash withdrawals can be made from ATM machines free of charge, both the bank's own and those belonging to other banks. Withdrawing cash over the counter at a branch will incur a fee of £2. More surprisingly, so will depositing cash or a cheque into an account at a branch counter. Customers may also make deposits at branches of Lloyds TSB, which will incur a £3 fee. These fees will be waived for customers who maintain an average balance of £1,500 per month in their current account or £5,000 in a savings account, which a customer on an average salary is unlikely to do. All banks are now moving towards discouraging customers from visiting branches in person, because they wish to reduce the costs involved in staffing branches at the level necessary to deal with large numbers of personal visitors, but the IBB seems to be out in front in the level of disincentive it is prepared to impose. The fact that an Islamic bank is severely restricted in the ways in which it can invest deposited funds and therefore in the profit it can generate from investment means that it is more reliant on fees from customers for its income. This is the negative aspect of the complete independence of the IBB from any *riba*-based institutions.

Other charges made on its current accounts, such as £30 for a returned cheque or £15 for a letter about 'mismanagement', are more in line with those charged by conventional banks, although higher than some; for example, the returned cheque fee charged by Lloyds on both its Islamic and conventional accounts is only £20. There is no authorised overdraft facility on the IBB current account. Of course, customers do sometimes overdraw without authorisation, and an Islamic bank cannot charge interest on these amounts as do conventional accounts. Instead, the IBB charges a flat fee of £30 for each cheque which cannot be refused because it is backed by the bank's cheque guarantee card, but which puts the customer's account into debit. Again, this is higher than its competitors' fees.

The IBB's annual report for 2009 states that the number of its customers has increased by 6 per cent to 50,000. This does not distinguish between holders of current accounts, savings accounts and home purchase plans. A newspaper report of the same year mentioned an increase in the number of accounts of 9 per cent to 74,000.[4] Of course, it is likely that many customers will hold more than one account.

The IBB's *shari'a* supervisory committee, which has approved the current account, consists of Abdul Ghuddah of Egypt, Nizam Yaquby of Bahrain and Abdul Barkatulla of Britain. Muhammad Taqi Usmani, now retired, was involved with the IBB in its early days.

Lloyds TSB

Lloyds TSB entered the Islamic sector of the market in February 2005 when it launched an Islamic current account.[5] Despite the fact that both HSBC and IBB were by then offering *shari'a* compliant accounts, Lloyds' director of current accounts issued a press release defiantly asserting that British Muslims were having to compromise their principles because 'their banking needs were largely uncatered for'. The appearance of this kind of straightforward competition between two high street banks and a specialist provider was encouraging to those sympathetic to the development of an Islamic finance industry, an indication that the Muslim market was regarded as worthy of the banks' competitive efforts and a sign that British Muslims would now be able to choose their bank on the normal criteria of price and convenience and not merely be expected to feel grateful for any Islamic options offered.

Possibly as a result of entering the market later and having to compete for customers with established products, the quality of the information provided by Lloyds about their Islamic accounts is very good. The provision of clear, thorough and easily understood explanatory material about the functioning of Islamic financial services is not always taken seriously enough by providers. This issue will become more important as the range of Islamic accounts available grows, and banks can no longer rely simply on being *halaal*, but have to compete with similar products on the basis of their standard of service.

Banking with Lloyds TSB offers the same balance of pros and cons as HSBC in terms of the accessibility and security of a major high street bank having to be weighed against the lack of independence of an Islamic window in a large conventional bank. Again, the Lloyds current account offers the usual facilities of a cheque book, debit card, standing orders and direct debits, and all routine transactions are free if the account is in credit. There is no credit or debit interest paid and no authorised overdraft facility. If an overdraft is created by a payment that cannot be stopped, the bank will charge a monthly 'management fee' of £15, but no interest will be charged on the debit balance.

Lloyds TSB is the only bank to offer an Islamic current account for students. This looks like an astute move, given the youthful profile of the British Muslim population and also the large number of Muslim students from overseas who attend universities in the United Kingdom. The account is, in fact, almost identical to Lloyds' conventional student account, with the addition of a promise that the funds will be managed in a *shari'a* compliant way. It offers free membership of the Youth Hostels Association as an incentive. Students who open an Islamic account are also entitled to all the other benefits available on the conventional student account, such as a free music downloading service, but the bank, mindful presumably of the disapproval of music by some scholars, adds cautiously that these other benefits are not *shari'a* approved.

The Lloyds Islamic student account is the only Islamic current account which offers an authorised overdraft facility. This is possible because Lloyds offers interest-free overdrafts of up to £1,500 to all students. The provision of free loans to students in this way is common practice at all the major British banks, who see it as a way of creating loyalty among young customers who will probably go on to earn higher than average salaries, but Lloyds seems to be the only bank to have realised that this custom could be given an Islamic interpretation. The fact that other student accounts do not offer the promise of *shari'a* compliant investment of the funds makes them unacceptable to the most observant Muslim students. Holders of Islamic accounts are also eligible to apply for a student credit card, but the bank, of course, makes it clear that this is not approved by their supervising scholars.

The *shari'a* supervisory committee at Lloyds, which has

approved these accounts, consists of four scholars rather than the more usual three. They are Nizam Yaquby, Imran Usmani, Abdul Barkatulla and Muhammad Nurullah Shikder. The last two are both British. Their names are prominently displayed in the section on the Islamic account in the booklet that covers all the bank's student services. It is encouraging that Lloyds does not feel any need to hide away the information on its Islamic account in a separate leaflet for fear of deterring non-Muslim enquirers.

United National Bank

This is a bank which caters mostly for British Pakistanis, and offers both conventional and Islamic services.[6] When it introduced its Islamic current account it allowed existing customers to convert a conventional account into an Islamic one without needing to change their account number or their chequebook. On the other hand, it also permitted customers to open a new Islamic account and continue to run the conventional one alongside it. The Islamic account does not pay interest or allow overdrafts. In the case of unauthorised overdrawing it will send a 'courtesy reminder letter' and charge for this. All the banks get around the problem of how to penalise an overdraft which cannot officially exist by charging some kind of fee, but they vary in the way this fee is described. It would appear to be difficult to overdraw on the UNB current account, however, as it does not provide either a debit card or a cheque guarantee card (neither does the UNB non-Islamic account), and might therefore be considered as not entirely adequate for the modern world. Both Islamic and conventional UNB accounts rely on using HSBC machines for cash withdrawal.

The UNB offers a more convincing case for the separation of its *shari'a* compliant funds from non-compliant ones than the larger mixed banks. It says that it uses the money deposited in its Islamic accounts to fund its Islamic home purchase plan. This seems to offer the nucleus of a completely self-contained Islamic division, and also gives depositors the satisfaction of knowing that their money is being used for the worthwhile cause of enabling more British Muslims to buy homes in a compliant manner.

This account has been approved by a single scholar, Abdul Barkatulla, a British imam trained in Deoband, India, who is actively involved in British Muslim affairs. As mentioned above, he also advises Lloyds and IBB.

Savings accounts

The difference between a cheque account and a savings account is that savings are placed on deposit over a longer term with the expectation of the capital increasing. For non-Muslims this increase is achieved through the payment of interest. Muslims seek to avoid interest, but still be paid a return in some form. The religious issue here is that since savings earn a reward the capital cannot be guaranteed. There must always be some stated risk of the loss of the capital, however remote and theoretical that risk may be. Here there is a direct clash with the FSA, which obliges all registered banks and other providers of money deposit facilities to implement its deposit guarantee scheme. The amount covered by this scheme was increased in the wake of the high profile bank failures of recent years, and at the present time it covers the first £50,000 of a customer's funds. Deposits up to this amount are guaranteed to be repaid in full even if the bank should fail, by government intervention if necessary. A bank which is authorised by the FSA (and all of the Islamic providers described in this chapter are authorised by it) cannot legally refuse to offer this guarantee, and so in order to make an account *shari'a* compliant the customer is usually given the option of waiving their entitlement to it.

Instead of interest being paid on the funds in a *shari'a* compliant account, a return is generated from investment. All customers' deposits are pooled and invested in *halaal* investments by the bank, and the profit is divided between the bank and the customer in accordance with a previously declared ratio. This is therefore a form of *mudaraba* contract. Strictly speaking, these accounts are known as 'profit-and-loss-sharing accounts', but the risk of any loss is remote. The profits are placed in a reserve fund by the bank and a fairly constant figure paid to the customer. This figure is described as a 'target profit rate' and usually tracks conventional interest rates closely. Differences in the performance of the investment over time are thus smoothed out and a reserve created to cover any period when the investments do in fact make a loss. Risk is additionally reduced by choosing very safe investments. Sometimes, in fact, the investment is simple commodity trading.

This difference from conventional interest paying savings accounts has created some issues with taxation. Interest payments are liable only to personal income tax. Originally the payment of profit to the holder of a profit-and-loss-sharing account was treated as if it were a dividend payment on company shares, and it was therefore liable to a tax levied on dividends known as 'corporation tax'. Legislation in 2005 removed this liability from profit-and-loss-sharing savings accounts and confirmed that the profit from such accounts should be taxed as if it were interest. Moreover, a bank which invests its customer's money in accordance with the latter's instructions is considered to be engaging in portfolio management, and in that case the bank's trading activity will be liable to 'value added tax' (VAT). Her Majesty's Revenue and Customs (the taxation department) has now confirmed that if the bank invests the money without consultation with the customer, which is the case with this type of profit-and-loss-sharing account, then the trading activity is not liable to this tax.

There are fewer high street banks offering Islamic savings accounts than current accounts. Lloyds and HSBC do not offer them at the present time.

United National Bank

The United National Bank (UNB) offers Islamic savings accounts for fixed terms of three, six and twelve months, and an open-ended account where the money can be withdrawn after giving ninety days' notice. In accordance with the principles of *mudaraba*, the rate of profit cannot be fixed in advance, but the percentages of the profit retained by the bank and paid to the account holder must be. The current version of the terms and conditions for these accounts states that the bank's share will not exceed 45 per cent for the ninety-day notice account, 50 per cent for the three-month term account, 47.5 per cent for the six-month term and 40 per cent for the twelve-month term. In other words, the share of profit awarded to the account holder increases if the money is left on deposit longer, in a way similar to the payment of higher rates of interest on conventional accounts. A maximum of 20 per cent of the customer's profit is retained in the 'profit stabilisation reserve fund'. The bank also deducts a fee for its services as *mudarib* of a maximum of 1.5 per cent of the total deposited funds. The profit is calculated monthly, but paid at the end of the term of the deposit (or monthly for the notice account).

If the investments in which the funds are deposited should make a loss, the bank states that it will withdraw funds from the 'profit stabilisation reserve' and may also waive its own fee. If this is not enough to make up the shortfall, it will offer to repay the money from its general funds, as required by the FSA, but gives customers the option of refusing to accept this money. The scholar who approved these accounts, Abdul Barkatulla, has given it as his opinion that anyone who does accept this offer of repayment will not be acting in accordance with *shari'a*. These are the legal niceties provided in the detailed information available on the bank's website. The most recent promotional leaflet for the bank's 'Islamic deposits', picked up in the Birmingham branch in June 2010, takes a less subtle view. It lists as the third of the key features of the accounts that there is 'no loss to capital'. This statement is almost certainly non-compliant.

Islamic Bank of Britain

The Islamic Bank of Britain has a large range of savings accounts, and is far ahead of any of its competitors in this area. It offers term deposit accounts for three, six, twelve, eighteen and twenty-four months, a sixty-day notice account, an instant access or 'on demand' account, an account which is only available online and a children's savings account. It is the only bank to offer a *shari'a* compliant account for children, and this could be an important factor in creating loyalty among future generations of British Muslims. When the child is fourteen they are permitted to operate the account themselves, and when they reach sixteen it is automatically converted into an adult savings account. The IBB also offers a treasury deposit account. The minimum investment in this is £50,000, and so it can more appropriately be dealt with in Chapter 9.

The fixed term deposit accounts employ a *wakala* or agency model, the other three accounts use *mudaraba* contracts. The bank's fee as *mudarib* is 1.5 per cent of the total funds deposited, averaged over the calculation period (one calendar month). The proportion of profit retained in the 'profit stabilisation reserve' fund is not more than 20 per cent of the 'net income', presumably the customer's income, not the profit before division. The bank's share of the profit is 50 per cent for the 'on demand' and 'young person's' accounts and 40 per cent for the online account, in line with the practice of conventional banks of offering higher rewards on online accounts because they are much cheaper to administer. For the fixed term accounts the profit rates are described as 'expected' rather than 'target'. The bank's fee as *wakeel* or agent is a nominal £1, simply to create a legal agency contract. Under this arrangement the bank retains the profits made on the investments above the amount the customer 'expects' to be paid.

An HMRC document[7] that deals with the tax treatment of Islamic savings accounts specifically discusses *wakala* as raising the same issues as *mudaraba*. One has the impression that the rather free use of Arabic terminology by some Islamic providers may not be helping the campaign for equitable treatment by the agencies of the state.

The issue of the conflict between the Islamic principle of reward being dependent on risk and the FSA deposit guarantee scheme is dealt with in the most recent editions of the 'terms and conditions' leaflets for IBB savings accounts, available in branches. These state that 'if the pool of funds referable to your capital returns a loss', the bank will offer to make good the amount of the shortfall, as they are required to do so by current UK banking regulations, but that the guidance offered by the *shari'a* supervisory committee is that anyone who does not exercise their option to refuse this offer will not be complying with *shari'a* principles.

The bank's annual report for 2009 states that its deposits are up 18 per cent on the previous year and have now reached a total of £186.6 million. It also mentions that the

yields produced by investing deposits in the Islamic inter-
bank market have fallen to historic lows. Certainly, the rates
of profit paid to account holders are currently very low,
in line with the very low rates of interest paid on conventional accounts. The highest is 2 per cent on the twenty-
four month fixed term deposit account. This does though
raise the question of whether the returns on profit-and-loss-
sharing accounts have anything much to do with genuine
investment, rather than with tracking interest rates.

On 2 December 2009, IBB's twenty-four month fixed
term deposit account, then offering 4.5 per cent return, featured as a lead story on the Yahoo UK website. It was a story
in the 'money' section of the site, but was also included as
one of the main featured stories on the 'home' page. Yahoo
is a web portal site aimed very much at a mass readership,
and so the prominence given to this product represents
significant recognition by the mainstream market.

The article stated that this rate of return was higher
than that available anywhere else, and was a very attractive
option for non-Muslims too. It explained the fact that this
is not interest but a return on investment, a 'target profit
rate' that the bank claims it has to date always achieved.
This non-Muslim writer commented that: 'handing your
savings over to be gambled on investments that you have
no idea about sounds suspiciously like what started the
whole banking mess in the first place'. I am sure that this
interpretation would grieve the promoters of non-interest-
based finance; in particular, the use of the word 'gambled'
is cruelly ironic, since the avoidance of gambling is central
to Islamic financial philosophy. The writer goes on to con-
clude that although the account is 'a little bit of a gamble'
it is a great option for anyone prepared to take this risk
in order to achieve a higher than average return on their
savings.

This article conveniently illustrates the difficulties of extending the market for Islamic products to non-Muslims. It displays the widespread confusion over the principle that profit on investment must accompany risk and cannot be guaranteed, which can superficially be interpreted as promoting speculation or even gambling. It also demonstrates the difficulty of adhering to this principle in a competitive banking environment where customers are, in practice, extremely reluctant to accept losses. The only way to attract customers who are neither committed Muslims nor particularly interested in ethical practices is to offer a higher rate of return than the secular competition, and this constantly leads the bank to the brink of offering a return which is illegitimately guaranteed.

Bank of London and the Middle East

The Bank of London and the Middle East (BLME) is concerned mostly with large-scale asset management and corporate banking, but it does offer a personal deposit facility, albeit one that will attract only those Muslims who come into the category of 'high net worth individuals', as the minimum deposit is £50,000. The account is available in euros and US dollars as well as sterling. The fixed terms of deposit available are three, six, nine, twelve, eighteen and twenty-four months. The 'anticipated profit rate' on £50,000 in a twenty-four month fixed term deposit account is currently 4 per cent.[8] The BLME describes this account as employing 'the Islamic Finance principle of Agency', without using the Arabic word *wakala*. It is perhaps noteworthy that the only bank which can realistically expect a large number of Arabic speakers among the customers for its personal deposit facility is the only one to avoid altogether using Arabic vocabulary in its English-language marketing.

Since the deposit guarantee scheme of the FSA only covers deposits up to £50,000 for any one customer in any one institution, there is no need to seek a waiver from those fortunate individuals who deal entirely in amounts above this figure.

National Savings and Investments

National Savings and Investments (NS&I) is a public sector provider of savings products. It is supported by the UK Treasury and its remit is to offer the public a safe and accessible form of saving while helping to make funds available to the government. NS&I uses post office branches for its counter transactions and pays more attention to lower income customers than do commercial providers. In 2008 it produced a very interesting review of the possibility of adding an Islamic product to its range, a report[9] that shows a thorough grasp both of the principles and workings of Islamic financial services and of the challenges of introducing them in the British market.

The biggest obstacle to NS&I introducing a *shari'a* compliant savings product is that the NS&I brand is based on guaranteeing the absolute safety of deposits. All their publicity declares prominently that there is a 'one hundred per cent' guarantee that you will get your money back. For an account to be *shari'a* compliant such a guarantee cannot, of course, be offered, because of the principle that any account which offers a return must bear some risk of loss. The introduction of an account which would have to be described as bearing such a risk of loss is thought to risk damaging the NS&I brand as a whole, by confusing non-Muslim customers and perhaps leading some of them to believe that none of the accounts offered are completely secure. The only way around this is believed to be giving Muslim customers the option of waiving the deposit guarantee imposed on all savings providers by the FSA, in the same way as the providers described above do.

Another source of concern to NS&I is that introducing a new Islamic product might simply create 'churn' in the market, that is, it would attract customers of other Islamic providers to move their accounts, rather than genuinely increasing overall demand. Because NS&I is a government-run organisation and well aware of the Treasury's desire to strengthen the Islamic finance industry in the United Kingdom, it does not want to take business away from other providers. In this its approach is fundamentally different from that of the banks, for whom enticing customers away from commercial rivals is the whole point of the exercise.

The writers of this review show a clear-sighted awareness that even a *shari'a* compliant product can be successful only if it offers a competitive return, and they believe that such a return could be sustained only if the account could attract more customers than simply Muslims. They hope that it could be 'dual positioned' as both Islamic and ethical, because the wider ethical finance market is a large and growing sector. The review eventually concludes that such dual positioning is not feasible. (A general discussion of the issues involved in promoting Islamic finance as part of the wider ethical finance movement is included in the final chapter.)

This consideration of the possibility of adding an Islamic savings account to the NS&I range was closely related to the Treasury's intention to introduce *sukuk*, an Islamic alternative to government bonds. The plan was that the returns on savings would be generated in a *shari'a* compliant form by linking the deposit account to the underlying asset of the *sukuk*. To date, however, the Treasury has not proceeded with its plan to issue *sukuk*, and so the NS&I *shari'a* compliant account is on hold until it does.

Notes

1. *British Muslims Monthly Survey*, August 1999. This report features a comment from Vince Cable, not then as well known as the Liberal Democrat finance spokesman as he is now, expressing disapproval of banks taking advantage of customers' refusal of interest to 'boost their profits'.
2. All the information on HSBC products in this chapter was taken from www.hsbc.co.uk/amanah, as of 1 June 2010. It has proved to be difficult to obtain figures for the number of Islamic accounts held at HSBC. They do not appear to be listed separately in any form available to the public.
3. All the information about IBB products in this chapter was taken from www.islamic-bank.com, as of 1 June 2010, unless stated to have been found on a paper leaflet in-branch.
4. 'London leads in race to be Western hub', *The Financial Times*, 8 December 2009.
5. The information about Lloyds products in this chapter was taken from www.lloydstsb.com/current_accounts/islamic_account, as of 1 June 2010, and from the in-branch leaflet about student accounts being distributed in the same month. Figures for the number of Islamic accounts held do not appear to be available to the public.
6. All the information about UNB products in this chapter was taken from www.unbankltd.com, as of 1 June 2010, except for the reference to the in-branch leaflet. The terms and conditions leaflets can be downloaded from the website. The most recent annual report available is for 2008 and does not show separate figures for Islamic accounts.
7. www.hmrc.gov.uk/manuals/vatfinmanual/VATFIN8500.
8. All of these details were found on www.blme.com, as of 1 June 2010.
9. *National Savings and Investment (NS&I) Sharia'a Compliant Savings Review*, June 2008. This document can be downloaded from www.nsandi.com.

CHAPTER 4
PERSONAL FINANCE

Islamic versions of personal loans are based on the Quranic principle that 'God has permitted trade but forbidden usury' (2:275). They are structured as sale contracts with the bank's profit being conceived as a return on legitimate trade rather than as the receipt of a time penalty for the customer having deprived the bank of the use of the money for a period, as with interest.

There is a shortage of ways of advancing cash to individuals at a profit in an Islamically acceptable form. Any institution prepared to do it in a non-profit making form, that is, as a *qard hasan*, will have the blessing of its advisory scholars but probably not of its shareholders. Companies also have serious problems in meeting their short-term liquidity needs in a *shari'a* compliant way; this is usually cited as the biggest obstacle to the growth of the Islamic finance industry. However, companies which trade on a large scale are more likely to be able to access acceptable ways and means of providing liquidity. The replacement of interest-based small personal loans is a keenly felt omission in the provision of *shari'a* compliant finance in the United Kingdom. Most of the banks that have found it worth their while to offer home finance have not felt able to introduce personal finance facilities for their retail customers. Perhaps the problem is that the only customers to whom the banks would be prepared to lend in these risk averse times are rich enough to have no need for the facility.

The Islamic Bank of Britain

At the time of writing the only bank in the United Kingdom offering a *shari'a* compliant personal finance facility is the IBB.[1]

The first thing that catches the eye of the enquirer after personal finance at the IBB is the strict limit on the type of customer who qualifies. Only people who own their home and have an income of at least £35,000 per annum will be accepted. This figure is well above the average national salary, which is around £25,000. The guidelines also specify that this income must be verifiable from payslips, which would appear to exclude the self-employed. It was noted in Chapter 1 that a higher proportion of British Muslims than of the general population are self-employed. The minimum amount which can be advanced is £5,000, which is somewhat more than many customers will need. A conventional bank might justify this rather high minimum for a loan by saying that smaller amounts could be covered by an overdraft or credit card, but neither of these facilities is available from the IBB. So a British Muslim on the average wage who needs a small cash advance for the purchase of a cheap second-hand car or some new kitchen equipment will, at least in the present economic climate, have to look elsewhere.

The IBB's personal finance facility is described as making use of the principle of *murabaha*, a term which normally describes a contract in which the goods are bought by the banks and resold to the customer at a higher price. The certificate of compliance signed by the *shari'a* supervisory committee, which consists of Abdul Ghuddah, Nizam Yaquby and Abdul Barkatulla, states simply that this facility is in accordance with the principle of *murabaha* and is therefore compliant. The detailed documentation about the facility, however, indicates that it employs a structure sometimes referred to critically as a synthetic *murabaha*, but more correctly known as *tawarruq*. Unlike a straightforward *murabaha* contract, in a *tawarruq* contract a third party must be involved in the sale and purchase to make them truly independent of each other. The bank and the customer cannot just buy and sell the goods to each other, and still less can the bank sell the goods to itself. The buying and selling is done by an agent. The goods that are the object of the sale are usually some kind of widely traded commodity, most often metals, because there is a large volume of short-term trading of metals on commodity exchanges.

Information available on the IBB's website states blandly that '*murabaha* is a special type of sale where the seller has to reveal to the buyer in advance the costs and profit being made on the transaction'. This formula does not explain anything about the distinctive structure of a *murabaha* agreement, and, while it may be true that in a normal sale situation the buyer is not aware of the exact profit being made by the seller, it is difficult to understand in what sense a conventional bank does not explain in advance the costs to the borrower and the profit to the bank of an interest-based loan.

In the case of a classical *murabaha* contract, the bank takes real possession of the actual goods that the customer desires to obtain, before reselling them to the customer at a higher price. In the case of a holiday or university fees, which are included in the IBB's examples of suitable subjects for its personal finance facility, there are no physical goods of which to take possession. This personal finance facility is really a way of generating cash, and it does this through the purchase and resale of 'commodities', the nature of which is unspecified except for a promise that they will be *halaal*. In the detailed documentation of the contract, it is explained that the customer appoints the company Dawnay Day & Co as his or her agent. The bank purchases some commodities and immediately sells them to the customer. The agent immediately sells them on behalf of the customer to a buyer. The agent deposits the funds received from the buyer in the customer's account. The customer pays the original purchase price of the commodities to the bank in instalments. The sale and purchase agreements are separate contracts which must be signed by the customer.

The booklet in which all this is explained, 'Personal Finance Terms and Conditions', consists of sixteen detailed pages, and while this satisfies the legal requirement to explain fully the contracts entered into, it is debatable how many customers would actually read or understand it in full. In practice, it is the endorsement by the supervising scholars on which customers rely for reassurance that the facility is *shari'a* compliant.

The *tawarruq* contract was used widely as an alternative to a conventional loan until in June 2009 it was ruled impermissible by the Fiqh Academy of the Organisation of the Islamic Conference. The scholars of the Academy took the view that the common use of *tawarruq* by banks today did not conform to the true classical form of this financing technique. The resulting exposure to accusations of non-compliance with *shari'a*, combined with the economic recession which was at its worst at the same time, made personal finance an unattractive market to enter. The IBB defends its use of *tawarruq* on the grounds that its advisory scholars regard it as still preferable to 'conventional personal finance principles', presumably meaning interest-based loans. It also states that it is more suitable than classical *murabaha* for the purchase of services rather than goods, and for situations where payment must be made to multiple parties, such as in the case of building a house extension.[2]

Credit cards

The question of whether a credit card can ever be *halaal* is intensely controversial. Some Muslims take the view that a conventional credit card is acceptable if the balance is paid off in full each month so that no interest charges are incurred. Others believe that the fact that the contract into which one has entered with a conventional credit card is based on the charging of interest makes it *haraam* even if one does not personally pay interest.

It could be argued that credit cards are not necessary at all. There are two aspects to their usefulness: the supply of credit and the facility to pay by card. The latter is becoming essential in the modern world. It is almost impossible to manage without some form of payment card now that so many purchases are made over the phone or Internet. There are though other forms of payment card which do not involve *riba*. Debit cards, where the payment is deducted directly from the customer's current account, are perfectly acceptable and do not raise any *shari'a* issues. Charge cards which require the full balance to be paid every month, such as American Express, are also acceptable in principle.

The recent appearance of a wide variety of prepaid cards also offers a *halaal* solution to someone who just needs a convenient way of paying for things. Many companies are now offering branded Mastercards where money is loaded on to the card in advance. They do not offer any credit interest. Many professionals would not regard these cards as meeting their needs, however, since they are aimed mainly at young people and tend to have designs that reflect this, and, because they are identifiably not credit cards, if produced at a hotel reception desk would raise questions about the user's credit worthiness. In many situations in the modern world there is pressure to be able to hand over a card that clearly represents a statement of confidence by a major bank in the user's financial status. For some high net worth individuals who do not need credit, this is in fact the main purpose of credit cards. Wealthy Muslims require a card that indicates piety but not poverty.

Meanwhile, of course, less advantaged customers actually need the credit element of a credit card. They want credit cards because they do not have sufficient income to pay the full cost of goods and services at the time of purchase. A large number of British Muslims are trying to get by with a level of income that usually excludes people from more advantageous offers of credit and makes them vulnerable to being forced into forms of borrowing with very high interest rates. It may well be that their avoidance of *riba* protects British Muslims from social pressure to borrow money in order to keep up an artificially high standard of living. In this sense the appearance of *shari'a* compliant credit cards may not be an entirely good thing for British Muslims. Certainly, some of the objections to the whole concept by scholars have been based on the argument that the culture of living beyond one's means is questionable in Islam, regardless of whether a credit card can be made technically compliant with Islamic rules. In some developing countries poorer people may need to use interest-based credit to pay for necessities such as health care and education, and some scholars regard this as justifiable on the grounds of *darura*, necessity, or *maslaha*, the public good. Since the British welfare state guarantees all the basic necessities of life to its citizens, through free health services and benefit payments to the unemployed or ill, the use of credit is almost always for the purchase of goods and services that cannot be justified on these grounds. The main exception is the funding of higher education, which is considered below.

Islamic banks which do issue credit cards usually make their profit by charging some form of fee for their use, rather than interest. The precise form the fees take and the way they are conceptualised Islamically vary.[3] The fees can be described as straightforward service charges, particularly if charges are made for the supply of paper statements or other peripheral aspects of the service. The charges can also be seen as the fee for the bank's role as guarantor for the customer's payment (the *kafala* model). Either way, these charges can often be higher than the interest charges on a conventional card. The *ijara*, or leasing, contract lends itself quite well to a credit card. The customer is regarded as only leasing the use of the assets purchased until all instalments on the payment have been completed. Or the card itself is a leased asset for which the customer pays regular 'rent'.

It is also possible to use some form of backwards version of a sale and mark-up contract, where the bank repurchases an item from the customer at a lower price than the latter paid. This can be a reverse *murabaha, tawarruq* or *bay' al'inah* contract. Some Islamic law schools regard the latter two models as identical, but others do not. In essence, all these models combine an instant sale by the customer with a deferred sale by the bank. The deferred sale takes place first, which is the 'reverse' aspect. The difference between the two prices forms the amount of credit available to the customer. This is the same principle as that used to provide a personal finance facility as a substitute for a conventional loan, described above, but is here used as a substitute for a conventional credit limit on a payment card. It is more difficult to use the deferred sale technique to generate cash for the customer to spend gradually as desired than to use it to purchase a particular item specified in advance. In the case of the purchase of a specified item, it is easy to see how a straightforward purchase and resale, or *murabaha*, contract works. In the case of a credit card, the sale and purchase are unrelated to the goods purchased with the credit and involve a third party to make them independent. Not only the *fiqh* scholars but the secular FSA have adopted a cool attitude towards *tawarruq*. Since it is not formally a loan, it is not covered by the FSA's regulation of consumer credit. This, combined with the administrative complexity and expense of these models, make it unlikely to be the preferred contract for *shari'a* compliant credit cards in the United Kingdom.

Traditionally, scholars have regarded it as unlawful to charge punitive fees in the case of default or late payment by the customer. This is a serious challenge to the commercial viability of credit products in the modern world. Some banks in the Muslim majority world describe these late payment fees as charitable donations, *sadaqa*, and pass them on to a philanthropic cause. The IBB donates late payment fees on its personal finance facility to charity. Its annual report for 2009 stated that it had paid £1,200 taken in late payment fees to charity on the recommendation of its supervising scholars.

To date, no Islamic bank in the United Kingdom has issued a *shari'a* compliant credit card. There have been rumours for some years that one might appear soon, and assertions that many British Muslims would be happy to have such a facility available. Despite the predictions of a healthy market demand, no bank has yet taken the plunge. The economic recession has caused a drastic restriction in the availability of credit by all banks, and the Islamic sector may well feel that it would be inadvisable to launch a radical new credit product at this time. In addition, it has continued to be difficult to persuade *shari'a* supervisory scholars of the acceptability of credit cards, particularly in a country where they are not really necessary. Banks based in the Arab world, Malaysia and Pakistan do offer *shari'a* compliant credit cards, and some Muslims in Britain may be in a position to obtain one of these. Once again, however, it is the more affluent and better connected Muslim, probably living in London, who will be in a position to take advantage of this.

HSBC is most likely to be the first bank to issue a credit card for the UK market. It already offers this product in other countries, so the model is well tested. In the United Arab Emirates (UAE) it offers cards that charge a straightforward monthly management fee. This fee may be waived or reduced if the customer spends a certain minimum amount that month and pays off the balance in full. This model has the advantage of giving the bank a way of managing customer behaviour without appearing to charge unlawful fees for late payment, as the incentive structure is based on withholding a discount rather than imposing an extra fee. The *fatwa* approving this product was signed by Nizam Yaquby, Muhammad Elgari and Imran Usmani, who are the same scholars who approve most Islamic financial services in the United Kingdom, so there is no religious obstacle to the introduction of the same model in this country.

If HSBC does make this credit card available through its high street branches in the United Kingdom, it would create mass availability of credit cards for British Muslims for the first time in the same way as its home finance plan opened up the market in *shari'a* compliant home purchase. It will not though do anything to change the basic problem that it is those who most need credit who are the least able to get it. While wealthy Muslims can access a product which claims to remove religious guilt from conspicuous consumption, those who are struggling to achieve a decent standard of living will have to seek credit wherever they can get it, which may be from exploitative 'loan sharks', or from 'ethical' schemes which seek to help the poor but do not meet technical standards of *shari'a* compliance, and so may still leave Muslims feeling religiously compromised.

Student loans

For the young professional, or aspiring professional, British Muslim, the dilemma of whether to take out an interest-bearing loan is particularly acute in the area of student fees and maintenance. In previous generations university students in Britain were supported entirely by non-repayable grants, which raised no *shari'a* issues, but for the last twenty years these have been replaced by loans.

It appears that possible difficulties for Muslim students with religious objections to interest-based loans did not register with the British government of the day (at that time Conservative) when loans were first introduced in 1990. In those days, of course, awareness in Britain of the Islamic financial tradition was much lower than it is today. The Labour Education Secretary, Charles Clarke, included the issue of student loans in discussions with the Muslim Council of Britain (MCB) in April 2004, seemingly at the latter's request. According to Iqbal Asaria, who was at the time the chair of the MCB's business and economics committee, no government representative had ever previously contacted them on this subject. The National Union of Students apparently recognised that Muslim opinion could be a powerful ally, since they once contacted the MCB to seek its support for a campaign against student loans. They appear to have been the only non-Muslim group to have approached the MCB on the subject of student loans on their own initiative.[4]

There is an established and respected body of scholarly

opinion that a rate of interest that merely keeps pace with inflation is not prohibited, because the purchasing power of the capital has not increased and it is the increase in the value of the capital which is the definition of *riba*. This is highly relevant to student loans, because the interest rate on them is fixed to match the rate of inflation as closely as possible. The interest rate varies from year to year according to information derived from the Retail Prices Index (RPI), the most widely used measure of inflation. The Student Loans Company explicitly states that because of this 'the amount repaid has the same value as the amount borrowed'.[5] In addition, since 1998 the repayment of student loans has been dependent on the borrower's income reaching a certain level, currently £15,000 per annum. If it has fallen below or never reached this threshold then the former student is permitted to defer repayments. Unlike any commercial loans, this accords with the Islamic principle that it is meritorious to allow a financially distressed debtor more time to pay, without penalty.

The distinction between the interest rates on student and commercial loans has become less marked over the last two years as the latter have fallen to an all-time low. Negative real interest rates have not significantly reduced Muslim opposition to interest-based savings accounts, which appears to be founded on the basic principle of interest, so it seems unlikely that interest rates no higher than inflation on student loans will persuade all Muslims that they are acceptable. There is also plenty of scope for anxiety in relying on the RPI for reassurance that the rate of inflation is the same as the interest on one's loan. The two figures can rarely be matched precisely, since the RPI reflects the past while the interest rate is fixed for the year ahead, and there are other measures of inflation in use which sometimes produce different figures.

There does not seem to have been any systematic study made of the attitudes of Muslim students and their parents towards methods of funding university study. A recent report[6] of a detailed research project carried out for the Department of Business, Innovation and Skills on students' knowledge of and attitudes towards loans makes no mention at all of any specifically Muslim concerns. The report includes a breakdown of participants by ethnicity and religion, and two of them (out of thirty-one) are described as Muslim, so presumably neither of these students raised any religious concerns during interview. There are some anecdotal reports of Muslim students refusing to take out loans, including those from hardship funds, because they are interest bearing. In some cases the opposition appears to come mostly from the parents, and it is possible that the issue is being used as a cover for a more general reluctance for their children, particularly daughters, to attend university.

Because of the vital role played by higher education in furthering the economic advancement and social integration of British Muslims, any obstacle to observant Muslims taking up university places must be of great concern. It is also possible that the situation could encourage the foundation of specialist Muslim colleges, where students are funded in other ways, which could be a positive development but could also produce an undesirable dependence on grants from overseas sources. Sadly, any government action on this issue is more likely to be spurred by the current panic over the alleged targeting of Muslim students by jihadist groups than by commitment to promoting equal participation in higher education.

Future possibilities

There will always be a limit to how much ordinary British Muslims can be helped with their short-term cash flow problems by large financial institutions who are unwilling to depart in any radical way from the policies governing conventional loans, in terms of the rate of profit they expect and their criteria of credit worthiness. In poorer communities the well-established non-Muslim tradition of credit unions has a valuable role to play. A credit union is a group of people who pay regular contributions to the union and in return are allowed to borrow from it. Credit unions are not run for profit and typically advance very small loans at a very low rate of interest. It is perfectly possible to run a credit union without charging interest at all, because the group chooses to make no profit on the loans or because any necessary reserve is covered by the required regular contributions. It is, therefore, a model which can be easily made *shari'a* compliant, and is in a sense a return to the joint savings schemes commonly run by early migrants to the United Kingdom.

One organisation that has attempted to develop the credit union model in an Islamic form is Ansar Finance,[7] founded in Manchester in 1994. Members of Ansar pay a compulsory minimum donation of £10 every month, and may pay more than the minimum if they feel able to do so. This contribution is always referred to as *sadaqa*, charity, not as a membership fee. After a year of making this payment regularly they become eligible for a loan 'for any halal purpose'. The original amount lent is repaid without any addition, while the monthly donations are maintained. It can be seen that even with this very low individual contribution, with, say, a thousand members (a figure which Ansar claims to have nearly reached), a large pool of money is created which can easily cover the small amounts of finance usually required by members. The fact that most members are linked through existing social networks creates a powerful sense of loyalty and disincentive to 'freeloading', and Ansar states that, although it has sometimes been necessary to extend repayment terms, it has never had a case of outright default. This is a model with tremendous potential. Unfortunately, Ansar seems to have become less active in the last few years. This seems to be due partly to increasingly onerous regulatory requirements, as the FSA has extended its reach over non-conventional forms of credit, and partly to the natural limit on the size of an organisation which depends on close social cohesion among members.

Some observers are sceptical of whether a community-based, non-profit making organisation of this type can ever be viable on a large scale.[8] This is part of a wider debate about whether idealistic, 'social enterprise' ventures have a serious role to play in the development of Islamic alternatives to the existing *riba*-based economic system, or whether the emphasis must be on making the Islamic alternatives commercially sustainable. It is evident that a model which gains its strength from existing community networks could not successfully be expanded to a bank with a national presence. What could perhaps work is many small local versions of Ansar.

Notes

1. All the information described as having been obtained from the website of IBB was found on www.islamic-bank.com, as it existed on 10 May 2010. The booklet 'Personal Finance Terms and Conditions' can be downloaded from this site.

2. Personal communication dated 18 May 2010 from Ghezala Sultan of the Islamic Finance Advisory and Assurance Services, who deals with media queries for IBB.

3. Paxford, Beata, 'Questions of price and ethics: Islamic banking and its competitiveness', *New Horizon*, April–June 2010.

4. The meeting with Mr Clarke was included in the electronic newsletter produced by the Muslim Council of Britain covering

the date 20 April 2004. The comment by Mr Asaria on the lack of previous government contact was made in a personal communication dated 9 March 2004, as was his reference to the approach by the National Union of Students.

5. www.slc.co.uk, accessed 29 April 2010.
6. Department of Business, Innovation and Skills, *The Role of Finance in the Decision- making of Higher Education Applicants and Students*, January 2010, available at www.bis.gov.uk.
7. www.ansarfinance.com.
8. 'Islamic mortgages: Shari'ah-based or Sharia-ah compliant?' and the following 'IIBI's point of view', *New Horizon*, January–March 2009.

CHAPTER 5
HOME FINANCE

The area of home purchase finance is by far the best supplied with *shari'a* compliant products in the United Kingdom. It accounts for the bulk of activity in the retail Islamic market.

Ahli United Bank

The Islamic Investment and Banking Unit of the Ahli United Bank was the first bank in the United Kingdom to introduce a form of *shari'a* compliant home purchase finance. This product was given the distinctive brand name of Manzil, an Arabic word meaning home or dwelling. For marketing purposes the Manzil Home Purchase Plan is promoted as a fairly self-contained product, with the Ahli name somewhat in the background.

Manzil was launched in 1997. At that time only a *murabaha* contract was offered. The basic principle of this is that the bank purchases a house on behalf of the customer and then resells it to the customer at a higher price. The customer pays the higher price in instalments in a similar way to the repayments on a conventional loan. The attraction of this form of finance to the bank is the simplicity of the contract in both conceptual and legal terms, and its close adherence to the underlying principle in Islamic law that the most acceptable type of contract is a straightforward sale contract. Title to the property is transferred to the customer immediately, which means that purchasers have the security of having the property registered in their own name and the bank does not need to worry about being caught by the legal responsibilities of landlords. It also offers both bank and customer clarity and certainty about the repayments, because the higher resale price is fixed at the outset and cannot be varied. To change the resale price part way through the repayment period would introduce a form of *gharar* into the transaction which would render it unlawful.

This inability to vary the repayment price can also become a disadvantage to either bank or customer, depending on what the financial and property markets do in the meantime. The difference between the two sale prices is set (by all banks which offer this facility) to approach as nearly as possible to the difference in the principal and repayment amounts of a conventional loan created by the addition of interest. In the United Kingdom it is usual to take LIBOR (London Inter Bank Offer Rate of interest) as the reference point for this price difference. Some thoughtful Muslims, both professional scholars and potential customers, are uneasy about this close relationship between a *murabaha* contract and an interest-based loan, and feel that it adds weight to the charge that a sale and mark-up contract is merely interest by another name. There are though no formal grounds to regard this form of home purchase finance as illegitimate.

One of the traditional criteria for the lawfulness of a *murabaha* contract is that the bank takes true possession of the item sold before reselling it to the customer. In the case of property purchase this presents much less difficulty than in the case of finance for the purchase of portable goods, where some physical movement of the goods may be felt to be a necessary part of taking possession. Taking legal possession of a house is merely a question of paperwork. This does, however, generate the biggest drawback to *murabaha* finance in the context of the English legal system, the fact that the necessity formally to transfer title to the property twice produces both additional lawyers' fees and, originally, a double liability to stamp duty land tax. As described in Chapter 2, this double tax liability was removed by the government in 2003. The matter of additional solicitors' fees remains though, and is aggravated by the shortage of solicitors qualified to practice in England who are expert in Islamic contracts, meaning that a lack of competition tends to keep fees high. It should be explained here that Scotland and England (with which Wales is included for legal purposes) have separate legal systems and lawyers qualified to practice in one jurisdiction are not automatically qualified to practice in the other. Manzil finance is available only in England and Wales. Lawyers qualified to practice in, say, the United Arab Emirates, or another country where Islamic contracts are much more common, cannot work in England without retraining. The legal skills needed for the successful functioning of Islamic finance are much less portable than the purely banking skills.

In 1999 Manzil added an *ijara* contract to the forms of home purchase finance available. This is a form of leasing contract. The bank buys the house and resells it to the customer at the same price. In addition to repaying this price in instalments, the customer pays rent to the bank for occupying the property while the bank owns it. Title to the property is not transferred to the customer until all repayments are completed, but the initial information provided by the bank avoids drawing attention to this fact.

These rental payments are set for a year at a time, in April. (The beginning of the financial year in England is 6 April, but the Manzil year runs from 1 April, presumably to avoid having to set rental payments for a fraction of a month.) They can be varied from one year to another. This ability to vary the repayments is an advantage to the bank in as much as it means that they can track the interest rate on conventional loans from year to year. This can, of course, also be an advantage to the customer if the interest rate has fallen since the date of initial purchase and the rental payments are lowered in conformity. The bank does not make much secret of the fact that rental payments, like the resale price with a *murabaha* contract, are set to reflect interest payments on a conventional loan rather than actual property rents. Apart from anything else, payments which genuinely reflected currently prevailing property rents would have to vary from one part of the country to another, and no bank would be eager to get involved with that degree of complexity. The bank's website runs a banner headline advertising its attractive rental rate, in a form almost indistinguishable from the way in which conventional banks highlight their competitive interest rates. 'Our new standard fixed Ijara Basic Rent rate until 1st April 2011 is now only 3.99%'.[1]

The other way in which the *ijara* model is much more flexible than the *murabaha* one is that it is possible for the customer to shorten the repayment period by making additional payments. The bank gives the customer the opportunity to make extra payments once a year, in April, before the payments for the next year are calculated. It is also possible for the customer to purchase the property outright at any time by repaying the original purchase price in full. The bank has found that this flexibility has made the *ijara* model much more popular than the *murabaha* one. In 2003 it was stated that 85 per cent of their customers for home purchase finance chose the *ijara* form.[2] One of the attractions is that making extra payments and thus reducing the future rent payable is an easy way to invest surplus funds productively for Muslims who have few *shari'a* compliant options for investment.

The maximum income multiple that Manzil will lend under a *murabaha* contract is two-and-a-half times a single salary, plus one times a second salary. Under a *murabaha* contract the maximum repayment term is fifteen years, which is much shorter than the usual maximum term for a conventional mortgage and means that monthly repayments are correspondingly higher. The maximum term of an *ijara* contract is twenty-five years, which is the usual term of a conventional mortgage, and the maximum income multiple available is three times a single salary, plus one times a second salary, which again is comparable to the amount usually offered under a conventional mortgage.

The Ahli Bank has now formalised their *murabaha* contract's lack of appeal to the ordinary British home purchaser, and states that it is available only to those who are buying property to let and to those who are not resident in the United Kingdom. It adds that title to the property can be registered in the name of 'Trusts, Corporates (offshore and onshore) and Partnerships'. *Ijara* finance is available to these groups, but it is also available to UK residents seeking to purchase their own home. The fact that it is available does not mean that it is affordable.

The amount of money available under either of the Manzil home purchase plans is not generous by the standards of the conventional mortgage market. Under both of the Manzil plans a maximum of 65 per cent of the purchase price can be obtained, leaving a 35 per cent deposit to be produced by the customer. During the period of steadily rising property prices before 2007, Ahli would lend up to 80 per cent of valuation, and this was considered cautious at a time when conventional banks would often lend 95 per cent or even 100 per cent of valuation. Now, during a period of recession and risk aversion, conventional banks have generally reduced their maximum to 80 per cent and Ahli (and other Islamic banks, discussed below) have reduced theirs even further. The fact that Islamic home finance providers have experienced far fewer problems with default than conventional mortgage providers has been mostly due, not to specifically Islamic factors, but to the fact that their lending criteria have always been very conservative. At the time of writing the average house price in the United Kingdom is around £170,000, so 35 per cent of this amount would be £59,500. This is somewhat more than twice the mean national salary. A typical young professional individual or couple would find it almost impossible to save up the deposit on a reasonably attractive home required under a Manzil plan. While it should be borne in mind that Muslims make more use of pooled family savings than most British homebuyers, the fact remains that British Muslims on average earnings are not the target market of Manzil home purchase plans.

HSBC

HSBC Amanah, the bank's Islamic division, launched a *shari'a* compliant mortgage for England and Wales in July 2003 in a blaze of publicity from the mainstream media as well as the Muslim press. At this time, property prices in Britain were soaring and making money from investment in property seemed to be easy. Conventional mortgage products were multiplying at bewildering speed and credit was easy to obtain on generous terms. In this atmosphere the non-Muslim media seemed to find the introduction of an 'Islamic mortgage' perfectly natural. The precise technical details of the Islamic contract tripped up some journalists, but the general idea that Muslims should not be excluded from participation in the national sport of buying and selling property found ready acceptance. The introduction of Amanah home purchase finance was the culmination of a long campaign by some British Muslims involved in the financial services industry to persuade major banks to enter the Islamic sector, but there is no doubt that the timing was influenced by the buoyant state of the housing market, which made an 'Islamic mortgage' appear to be a low risk venture.

The information booklet produced by HSBC for distribution in branches was called simply *HSBC Amanah Finance* and covered both the home purchase plan and the current account. Out of a total of twenty pages, two pages were taken up with the career details of the *shari'a* supervisory scholars and no fewer than seven pages consisted of photographs of desirable homes, both inside and out. One full-page exterior shot depicted a typically British house, a detached property rather than one of the small terraced houses in which so many British Muslims live, but unmistakable in its late nineteenth-century red-brick design with small front garden, a house that could not be in any other country. The juxtaposition of such images with details of Islamic law had previously been seen only in media coverage of adverse events in British cities with large Muslim populations. The publicity material for Amanah Finance placed British Muslims firmly in a consumer context. HSBC advertised heavily in a new magazine for British Muslims called *Emel*, subtitled *the Muslim lifestyle magazine*, which contained many illustrations of attractive homes, similar to those in the bank's own advertisements. There was an implicit message here of integration through consumption.

The version of the HSBC Amanah home finance booklet which is now being distributed is less specifically British than the first one. The illustrations show a Muslim family who could be in any country in the world. This is part of a general trend to standardisation and internationalisation in HSBC Amanah's services and also coincides with a reduction in the promotional effort being put into *shari'a* compliant services in the United Kingdom. The Amanah website is less separate from the main HSBC site than it used to be and there are fewer Amanah posters seen in branches.

The original form of the Amanah home purchase plan was a classic *ijara* model. The bank purchased the property, registered title to it in the bank's name and registered the buyer's tenancy. The latter would then make monthly payments to the bank consisting of rent plus a payment towards purchase of further equity. Once all payments had been completed the title would be transferred into the name of the buyer. The monthly payment also included a sum towards the cost of buildings insurance, which was taken out by the bank in its own name as the legal owner of the property. The information material provided was notably straightforward about the status of the homebuyer as a tenant – possibly unwisely so. As Islamic finance has become more widespread all banks have tended to become vague about the precise legal status of the homebuyer under an Islamic contract. There are significant legal implications in choosing to buy a home through an Islamic *ijara* contract rather than through a conventional loan. The form of redress available to the bank in the case of default by the customer would involve evicting the latter as a tenant rather than invoking the mortgage charge in order to take possession of the property, as with a conventional loan. In the case of a customer choosing to take out *ijara* finance with Amanah in order to repay a conventional mortgage loan, the decision to refinance would involve a change in their strict legal status from an owner to a tenant, which would usually be regarded as an undesirable move.

The status of the buyer as technically a tenant also created difficulties with the purchase of leasehold property, which was a considerable limitation of the market. In English law the majority of flats are held leasehold, that is, the owners of the individual apartments have to pay a nominal rent to the owner of the freehold of the building as a whole. The HSBC home purchase plan in its original form could be used for leasehold houses (which are rather uncommon), with the landlord's consent, but the information provided to customers stated clearly that 'the plan does not support the purchase of flats'. A large number of young people, particularly in London, find this type of property the most convenient and affordable, and so many young professional British Muslims must have been disappointed to find a clause in the glossy brochure handed out by their local HSBC branch stating that *shari'a* compliant finance was not available for flats.

On the positive side, Amanah was prepared to accept joint applications from up to six people for home purchase finance, which offered young people the alternative option of buying a shared house, as well as being suitable for extended families. Extra payments could be made under the *ijara* contract twice a year, with a minimum payment of £5,000, and the property could be purchased outright at any time by making repayment in full of the original price. In the happy days of 2003, HSBC was prepared to lend up to 90 per cent of the value of the property and allow a maximum repayment term of thirty years. In common with most other Islamic home finance providers, Amanah has become much more conservative about its exposure to changes in house prices and will now advance only a maximum of 65 per cent of the value of the property. It will still allow income multiples of three-and-a-half times the applicant's salary, which is fairly good in the present market.

HSBC has now switched to a diminishing *musharaka*

model for its Amanah home purchase finance.[3] This may have been influenced by the appearance of a new competitor in the British market, when Lloyds TSB launched its own Islamic home purchase plan (see below) which used the diminishing *musharaka* contract and was widely regarded as a preferable choice. In 2005, the exemption from liability to double stamp duty on Islamic home purchase plans was extended to *musharaka* structures in recognition of their addition to the options being offered by banks. With diminishing *musharaka* finance it is possible to purchase leasehold flats. The lease must have at least fifty years of the term left and the landlord's consent is required. Items such as ground rent and service charges, which are commonly payable by owners of leasehold flats, are paid by the bank and added to the buyer's monthly payments.

There is very little difference in the practical details of repayments of *ijara* and diminishing *musharaka* finance; both involve the payment of rent for the use of the share of equity still owned by the bank plus extra payments for the purchase of equity. In the case of *ijara*, the original sale price is repaid in instalments and ownership is not transferred until the whole of this price has been repaid. With *musharaka*, the property is jointly owned by the bank and the purchaser from the outset, with the proportions of the ownership held by the two parties gradually shifting as the purchaser makes payments. In theory this means that the homebuyer is never a tenant, and thus avoids the associated legal problems. In the case of HSBC Amanah the property being purchased is held in trust on behalf of both the bank and the buyer by HSBC Trust Company and outright title to it is transferred to the buyer only on completion of all payments. The trust comes into existence on the date of legal completion of the purchase and so does a tenancy in the name of the buyer. The precise nature of this joint ownership and partial tenancy arrangement and the implications in the case of default by the buyer have never been tested properly in English law. Reluctance to have the legal details picked over in court is probably an additional reason for the bank to be very cautious in assessing applications for home finance.

The *shari'a* supervisory committee of Amanah Finance at the time of its launch consisted of Muhammad Taqi Usmani of Pakistan, Nizam Yaquby of Bahrain and Muhammad Elgari of Saudi Arabia. Mufti Usmani, a renowned expert on Islamic banking who has made a great contribution to the development of the industry, has now retired from all his active involvement with Islamic financial institutions, and his place on the HSBC committee has been taken by his son, Imran Ashraf Usmani. The international nature of HSBC's business means that their *shari'a* advisory arrangements are also international, and these scholars all sit on the bank's central *shari'a* committee, which advises on business in many countries. The bank explains that it is seeking greater standardisation in the Islamic financial services industry and sees centralised *shari'a* supervision as helpful for this. This may be true, but it seems a pity that there is no British scholar involved in Amanah's business in the United Kingdom, a market which appears so promising and so innovative.

Al-buraq

Lloyds TSB bank introduced an Islamic home finance plan for England and Wales in February 2005. (Since this bank absorbed HBOS in 2009 it has reverted to calling itself simply Lloyds.) It was not the bank's own plan, but one created by the Arab Banking Corporation, whose UK subsidiary is ABC International Bank. The plan was called Al-buraq, which was already available in a number of other countries and marketed under that name as a stand-alone product. Al-buraq is the name of the winged horse that carried the Prophet on his miraculous journey from Mecca to Jerusalem. The Al-buraq company's own website shows a wing attached to the name and justifies its use to indicate a home purchase plan by describing the plan as 'a journey to a new type of financial service'.

To complicate matters further, ABC's partner in the United Kingdom was the Bank of Ireland, specifically Bristol & West plc, formerly an independent building society but now a division of the Bank of Ireland. In its publicity material Lloyds put a positive interpretation on the number of company names involved by describing them all as 'a great team' and pointing out that the plan had been approved by two separate *shari'a* committees, its own and that of ABC, which meant that customers could be 'doubly sure' that it was fully religiously compliant. The scholars on the Lloyds committee were Nizam Yaquby, Imran Usmani, Abdul Barkatulla and Muhammad Nurullah Shikder. Al-buraq's own committee consists of three of the same scholars (the one missing is Dr Usmani), so the double approval means little.

The Al-buraq plan uses a diminishing *musharaka* contract, where the buyer pays rent for the use of the proportion of the property owned by the bank and also acquisition payments to increase the share of the property that the buyer owns. The rents are set with reference to the LIBOR interest rate and reviewed twice a year. The property is owned jointly by the bank (Bristol & West) and the buyer 'although the title deeds will be in Bristol & West's name', with the title deeds being transferred into the name of the buyer after completion of the acquisition of the entire equity of the property. Lloyds says that the principle of the sharing of risk is at the heart of Islamic finance, and under a diminishing *musharaka* the bank (Bristol & West) and the buyer share the risk of the property gaining or losing in value, but the bank does not benefit if it gains in value. This sounds attractive, but in practice it is hard to see how the bank shares any more risk than does the lender under a conventional mortgage. An Islamic finance provider does not share the loss if a property loses value, since the initial acquisition cost must be repaid in full and the rents are unrelated to the value of the property, nor does a conventional lender benefit if a property increases in value, since the amount to be repaid is not increased. In addition, all banks have been anxious to avoid assuming responsibility for the maintenance of properties purchased under diminishing ownership schemes. Again, it would be interesting to see what a court made of this statement that the property is owned jointly despite the fact that the title deeds are in the name of only one party, but to date the opportunity has not arisen.

Originally, the bank would lend up to 90 per cent of valuation over a term of up to twenty-five years. The information supplied to enquirers is[4] commendably straightforward about the disadvantages of this form of home finance. It cannot be used to purchase council houses under the 'right to buy' scheme. (HSBC leaves customers to find this out for themselves later.) If the purchaser becomes unemployed state support may not be available to help with repayments in the same way as they would be with an interest-based mortgage, because the terms and conditions of the relevant benefit specify that it covers interest. (This is an issue which concerned the government committee on Islamic finance.) If the purchaser should die the payments will be covered only if he has chosen to take out non-Islamic life insurance. Lloyds believes (correctly) that there is no *shari'a* compliant form of life insurance available in the United Kingdom and does not insist that homebuyers take out non-compliant policies, but points out that if the buyer chooses not to do so then there is no certainty that his family will not lose their home in the event of his death. The same applies to non-compliant insurance against unemployment or long-term illness. The best the bank can do is to promise to 'act fairly and reasonably' and try to add the names of additional income earners to the contract. This form of wording about acting 'fairly and reasonably' is also used by IBB, but the latter is less clear about the full implications of default.

When it was first introduced, the Lloyds home finance plan was widely perceived as a more attractive product than the HSBC version, because it promised joint ownership of the property from the outset and because it was available for the purchase of leasehold flats. More generally, the appearance of real competition for Muslim customers among mainstream high street banks was welcomed. Sadly, in the United Kingdom Al-buraq fell victim to the recession in the form of a decision by the Bank of Ireland to reduce the extent of all of its mortgage liabilities. The Bank of Ireland, and therefore Lloyds, stopped accepting new customers for this product in May 2009, but are still honouring existing contracts. Both Lloyds and Al-buraq state that they are seeking a new partner to enable them to resume offering this product in the United Kingdom, and that the decision to withdraw it had nothing to do with any lack of success.

Islamic Bank of Britain

The Islamic Bank of Britain was founded in 2005, but did not introduce home purchase plans until September 2008. The promotional slogan for these plans is 'the halal mortgage alternative'. The colloquial use of the word 'mortgage' to refer to a loan for house purchase, rather than to the legal charge over the property held by the lender in a conventional arrangement, is so firmly established in British usage that no Islamic bank has felt able to dispense with the word altogether in its publicity material. An Islamic home purchase plan involves neither a mortgage nor even technically a loan, but insisting on this standard of precision in marketing terminology would make it very difficult for many potential customers to locate Islamic products, particularly on the Internet. The formula chosen by IBB can be read as offering either an alternative to a mortgage or an alternative form of mortgage, and can thus satisfy everyone.

The IBB's branding is very much that of a bank aimed at British Muslims. Its branches, its website and its leaflets are coloured in the distinctively British combination of red, white and blue, and it makes clear that its main language of operation is English (although it claims that it endeavours to cater for customers whose first language is not English by employing staff who speak community languages). After studying many Islamic home purchase plans one becomes accustomed to 'Britain' or 'the UK' translating in practice to 'England', but the IBB really does offer finance for the purchase of houses in Scotland as well as England and Wales. A plan adapted for Scotland was introduced in 2009, a year later than the English original. The structure of the finance appears to be identical, but applications for Scotland are processed separately because of the differences in the legal procedure involved in property purchase between the two countries.

The IBB describes[5] its home purchase plan as employing both the *ijara* and diminishing *musharaka* principles, although its structure is the same as that which other banks describe simply as a diminishing *musharaka*. It appears to be identical to the Lloyds plan and, indeed, Al-buraq states[6] that it helped the IBB when it was developing its home finance plan, although the IBB makes no reference to the Al-buraq name. The bank buys the property and the customer makes 'acquisition payments' for the gradual purchase of the equity, while also paying rent for use of the proportion of the equity still owned by the bank. The bank holds the legal title to the property until completion of repayments, but the customer will have 'the beneficial interest of the property' with a long leasehold registered in their name at the Land Registry. If the property is leasehold rather than freehold a sub-lease is registered in the customer's name. This does seem to give greater clarity and security to the buyer than ambiguous statements about joint ownership. In its explanation the bank stresses that this leasing structure is necessary to avoid the payment of interest and that in this way the bank enters into a real partnership with the buyer, sharing the responsibilities and risks connected with ownership of property. It is difficult to see how the bank shares these in any meaningful way, as it obliges the buyer to take out buildings insurance, and there is no suggestion that the bank will share the loss if the property falls in value by reducing the amount of finance to be repaid.

In the past IBB reviewed the rent element of the customer's payments half yearly, in March and September, but has recently changed to quarterly reviews, in March, June, September and December. It can alter the rent from the first day of the following month, although it promises to give thirty days' notice of any change. This means that the customer's repayments could in theory change every three months, which could make budgeting difficult. The bank explains that this frequency of review is made necessary by its dependence on its own depositors for funds. A self-contained Islamic bank cannot rely on borrowing in the wider markets to smooth its cash flow, but has to closely match funds coming in and funds going out in order to maintain a consistent profit margin.

The maximum term of repayments is thirty years, a fairly

generous length of time that could help to reduce payments, and IBB will consider joint applications from up to four people; that is, it will take into account up to four salaries in assessing the amount of finance it is prepared to grant, as long as all four of these earners both own and occupy the property. This could apply to a situation where parents and adult children share a property, an arrangement more common in the Muslim community than in wider society, or to a group of young people sharing a house while they cannot as yet afford individual properties. The bank refuses to describe its criteria for assessing applications in terms of a fixed multiple of salary being obtainable, but insists rather that they look at the wider picture of the customer's financial commitments to get a better sense of 'affordability'. This is in accordance with current ideas of good lending practice.

The maximum proportion of the value of the property obtainable is at the present time a dispiriting 60 per cent, much less generous than most conventional mortgage lenders and an insuperable barrier to many potential applicants for new purchases. The bank's information booklet *Home Purchase Plan* does not seem to have been updated to reflect new economic circumstances as it still illustrates the working of the plan with the example of the bank paying 80 per cent of the purchase price of the property, as it would do in more cheerful economic times. These home purchase plans can also be used to release capital from a property already owned or to transfer from a conventional mortgage product to an Islamic home purchase plan. This could be an attractive possibility for any Muslim whose house has increased enough in value in the years since the conventional loan was first taken out for 60 per cent of its current value to be sufficient to pay off the original loan. In the present recessionary climate this may in fact be the biggest market for these products.

A separate and more up-to-date leaflet giving summary details of the home purchase plan is available online and from dispensers in some branches. It begins with the opaque formula: 'Rent Rate = Base Rate + a margin of 4.25%, currently 4.75%' (as of January 2010). Further enquiry reveals that the base rate referred to is the Bank of England base rate of interest and this formula makes it as clear as it could be that rent payments are set to track interest rates. For some Muslims the form in which rent rates are quoted, as percentages, suggests interest rates so strongly that they cannot accept that the product can be truly Islamic. There are anecdotal reports of Muslims who were interested in applying for an IBB home purchase plan until they saw the bank's television advertisement, which gave prominence to what the bank believed was a competitive percentage rate and had the unfortunate effect of making some viewers less rather than more favourably inclined towards the product advertised. These doubts feature as one of the 'frequently asked questions' in the bank's information booklet. The answer is that 'to ensure that we give you a competitive price and to ensure that we are in line with the rest of the market we use the Bank of England base rate as a benchmark to ensure that our product is priced competitively with other products in the market'. This begs a lot of questions about whether an Islamic bank should use the rest of the market as a reference point at all, and provides much material for debate between purists and pragmatists about the appropriate strategy for an Islamic bank in a non-Muslim country.

The bank's *shari'a* supervisory committee consists of Abdul Ghuddah of Egypt, Nizam Yaquby of Bahrain and Abdul Barkatulla, based in Britain but trained in Deoband, India. Muhammad Taqi Usmani, now retired, was involved with IBB in its early days. IBB is to be congratulated for employing a British scholar to advise it. A large number of British imams are aligned with the traditions and philosophy of the Islamic college at Deoband. The committee's certificates of endorsement of all the bank's products are available on the website. The certificate approving the home purchase plan simply states that it 'is in accordance with the Diminishing Musharaka and Ijarah Principles of Islamic finance and therefore we allow the Bank to provide this product to its customers'.

The presentation of information about IBB's home purchase plan is not as clear as it could be. The bank's website is difficult to navigate and infrequently updated and the key points about the plan are scattered across several pages. This is important because the bank has chosen to rely heavily on online delivery of publicity material. When the writer asked to be sent copies of information leaflets about the bank's main products, the reply was that none were available, the bank's policy was not to send out paper information and that everything one needed to know was on the website. It is not strictly true that no paper information is produced, as leaflets are readily available in branches, but the amount of information provided on them is also limited and frequently out of date. The general policy of IBB is to encourage anyone with any interest in their home finance to telephone and request a personal illustration, rather than providing detailed general information at the initial point of contact, and their enquiry line is free, open long hours and staffed by friendly people. This may be a good marketing strategy in as much as it draws potential customers into active consideration of a personal plan at an early stage, and it may suit older customers who feel more comfortable finding out what they wish to know by means of a real conversation with a human being, especially if English is not their first language. It may though underestimate the desire of some enquirers to thoroughly understand the structure and details of the Islamic contract before proceeding any further.

United National Bank

The United National Bank is the British registered division of a Pakistani bank, and caters specifically to the needs of the Pakistani community in Britain. Its decor and its publicity material favour green, the colour of the Pakistani flag, and it claims that all its staff are bilingual in English and Urdu. It is not a wholly Islamic bank; it offers conventional mortgages as well as Islamic home finance, including a mortgage provided by its parent bank in Pakistan to British residents for the purchase of property in Pakistan. The UNB cheerfully refers to its *shari'a* compliant home finance as its 'Islamic mortgage', which reinforces the sense that it is just one mortgage option on the list. This creates an interesting difference from those banks which conceive the entire British Muslim community as their target market and use religious obligation as a marketing device. It means in effect that UNB is obliged to present *riba*-free finance as something that Muslims may care about but may also legitimately not care about.

The UNB home finance plan is available for the purchase of properties in Scotland as well as England and Wales. The bank has a branch in Glasgow, where the Pakistani community of Scotland is concentrated. It was, in fact, the first bank to offer Islamic home finance in Scotland, having introduced this in 2004, five years before IBB entered the Scottish home finance market. The UNB home purchase plan can be used as a form of refinancing to replace a conventional mortgage, it is available to non-residents and it is suitable for 'most types of property' including commercial premises. The bank indicates that it cannot be used for the purchase of social housing under 'right to buy' schemes.

United National Bank uses a pure *ijara* contract where title to the property remains with the bank until completion of all repayments. There is a maximum term of twenty-five years. The rental rate uses the Bank of England base rate of interest as a 'benchmark', and the bank states honestly that this is in order to ensure that it makes the same profit as other banks would on a conventional loan. The rent is reviewed at six-monthly intervals, but this frequency is liable to change. In the 'frequently asked questions' the bank addresses worries over rents increasing to a level that the customer does not feel comfortable with, but in reply offers only the unhelpful advice that if the customer objects to the new rent he has the option of ending the contract by paying off the sale price in full.

The information provided by the bank cites only a single scholar as the source of approval for its home finance plan: Imran Ashraf Usmani, who is based in Pakistan and is the son of the well-known Pakistani judge and leading expert on Islamic finance, Muhammad Taqi Usmani. It is unusual not to have a supervising committee of at least three scholars, but the status of this scholar and the standardised nature of the *ijara* contract probably render this redundant in this case, and dispensing with the services of another two scholars will certainly have saved the bank some money. The bank advises the customer to take independent *shari'a* advice from 'your local Imam or Mufti' and to ensure that the contract conforms to 'your own personal view of the Shari'ah'. Using a strikingly legalistic phrase, it says that 'United National Bank can accept no liability if you later discover that the UNB Islamic Mortgage does not meet with your interpretation of Shari'ah law'.[7] Of all the banks providing *shari'a* compliant home finance in the United Kingdom, UNB is the only one to make so explicit the necessity for the customer's own conscience to be the final arbiter.

The phrasing suggests that this emphasis is prompted by fears of litigiousness among customers subsequently racked by religious doubts (any resulting court cases would make interesting listening), but it is an approach surely more in keeping with the tradition in Islam that every Muslim should study and understand as much as possible about the religion than is the commonly found implication that the great eminence of the advising scholars makes independent judgement unnecessary.

The limitations of Islamic home purchase plans

The poor standard of information offered by some providers about the implications in English (or Scottish) law of Islamic home purchase plans has been a cause of concern to the FSA. It has not criticised any particular bank, but has expressed a general anxiety that those British Muslims who are most committed to their faith, and therefore to observing the principles of Islamic finance, may be the most vulnerable to agreeing to forms of contract that have the potential to disadvantage them in ways they do not fully understand, relying as they do on an implicit belief that anything Islamic must be fairer and safer than anything non-Islamic. In 2007, those products previously known colloquially but inaccurately as 'Islamic mortgages' were given the general designation of 'home purchase plans' (HPPs) and brought within the scope of the FSA's regulation of all forms of home purchase finance. In that year the FSA produced a survey of the Islamic financial sector that touched on some of these general concerns, and also a booklet about *ijara* home purchase plans in its series of 'money made clear' guides (aimed at improving public understanding of financial services) which gave prominence to the fact that the purchaser does not legally own the property until the end of the payment term.[8]

Some of what was said in Chapter 4 about personal finance also applies to home finance. For as long as the market is controlled by Islamic banks that use the same profit margins and criteria of credit worthiness as conventional banks, the mere fact that the form of financial assistance is Islamic cannot help poorer Muslims to achieve the ownership of their own home. In this respect the concern of the government to ensure that Muslims in social housing are not excluded from entering owner-occupation by a lack of availability of Islamic home finance plans is commendable but limited.[9] No Islamic provider presently in the UK market will give home purchase finance to people who are low earners, cannot provide a large deposit or have a poor credit history, any more than conventional providers will. Furthermore, if such poorer customers are able somehow to raise the finance to buy their own home, it will inevitably be a cheaper and therefore less desirable property, and this will perpetuate the pattern of high rates of ownership of poor quality housing noted in previous chapters. Difficulty in obtaining personal finance to fund home improvements will ensure that the condition of the property continues to deteriorate. Some writers who have studied the UK housing market have observed that a well-maintained council or housing association owned home is often preferable to owner-occupation of a decaying property, if one looks simply at the level of amenity offered. The most useful thing the government could do to improve the housing situation of the remainder of the British Muslim community, now that the more affluent have been provided with religiously compliant home purchase plans, is to increase the availability of good quality social housing in the regions where the Muslim population is concentrated. Because competition for council housing, construed in racial or religious terms by the disaffected, has been one of the main sources of recruitment to political groups who are explicitly hostile to Islam, this would also help to improve the social and political climate for British Muslims.

Alternatives to commercial home purchase plans

Ansar Finance, the Manchester organisation discussed in Chapter 4 in connection with personal finance, has a home purchase division called Ansar Housing. This is a membership organisation and anyone wishing to receive home purchase finance must first become a member and save up a deposit (originally 20 per cent of the purchase price) through regular contributions to the organisation's funds. Ansar Housing uses a diminishing *musharaka* contract. The difference from commercial providers of home purchase plans is that Ansar does genuinely share in the risks and rewards of ownership. If the property is sold at an increased value before repayments have been completed the profit is divided between the owner and Ansar. If the owner has purchased more than 50 per cent of the equity in the property Ansar will receive 10 per cent of the increase in value and if not Ansar receives 20 per cent. This share in the profit will be added to the organisation's funds and used to enable more people to purchase homes. Information on what happens when the property has fallen in value is not available, possibly because to date no member has sold a home in these circumstances, but the organisation is committed to supporting members in financial difficulty.

Ansar Housing operates on a very small scale. It has purchased only a very small number of houses and in recent years it has become less active. Many people involved in Islamic finance consider it to be excessively idealistic. Considered in a wider context, however, it is a model which could flourish in a convergence of Islamic and non-Islamic 'ethical' finance.

Such a convergence could see a revival of the British tradition of building societies. The original model for a building society is that it accepts deposits from savers and uses these funds to lend out to borrowers for the purpose of buying a home, without borrowing additional funds on the money markets and without having to worry about satisfying shareholders, because as a mutual society it is owned by its members, that is, its savers and borrowers. Over the last twenty years there has been a wave of demutualisation and conversion into banks by British building societies. Some of these demutualised organisations (most notably Northern Rock) fared very badly in the banking crisis of 2007–8, and this has led to a renewal of interest in the mutual model. Some creative thinking would be needed to make the mutual model work without using interest rates to balance deposits and borrowing, but in principle the concept of an organisation that has as its main goal helping its members to buy homes rather than making profit for its shareholders is in keeping with the spirit of the Islamic financial tradition. This is an area where the interaction of British and Islamic traditions could lead British Muslims to produce something truly innovative.

Notes

1. All the details described as having been taken from the bank's website are from www.iibu.com, accessed 10 May 2010.
2. Leach, Keith, 'Islamic home finance in the UK: structures, Barnes and market experience', *New Horizon*, June 2003.
3. All the information about the bank's current home finance plan can be found on www.hsbc.co.uk/amanah, accessed 21 May 2010. The booklet *Home Finance* can be downloaded from this site. The booklet *Amanah Finance* which was distributed in branches in 2003 is no longer available.
4. All this information is still, as of 21 May 2010, available on

the Lloyds website (even though the product is not currently available) at www.lloydstsb.com/mortgages/islamic_home_finance_faqs. The present situation was confirmed in a personal communication from the Lloyds media office on 5 May 2010.

5. All the details described as having been taken from the bank's website are from www.islamic-bank.com, accessed 10 May 2010.

6. www.alburaq.co.uk/homefinance_update, accessed 21 May 2010.

7. *UNB Islamic Mortgage*, p. 5. This booklet can be downloaded from www.unbankltd.com, accessed 21 May 2010.

8. Financial Services Authority, *Islamic Finance in the UK: Regulation and Challenges*, November 2007; Financial Services Authority, *Just the Facts about Home Purchase Plans*, September 2007, both available to download at www.fsa.gov. uk.

9. A perception by some Muslim tenants that the 'right to buy' scheme is worsening the housing situation of those unable to afford to buy is discussed in Sellick, Patricia, *Muslim Housing Experiences*, Housing Corporation, September 2004. This report can still be downloaded from www.housingcorp.gov. uk, even though the Housing Corporation has been closed down, or it can be obtained from the Oxford Centre for Islamic Studies, who undertook the research for it.

CHAPTER 6
TAKAFUL

Takaful is a word derived from an Arabic root with the basic sense of mutual assurance or solidarity. It does not translate directly as insurance, and the word has become established only relatively recently as the Islamic equivalent of insurance. The 1976 edition of the Wehr dictionary, the recognised standard Arabic–English dictionary (which mentions in a preface that a new edition was prompted by the great increase in interest in the language brought about by developments in the oil states in the early 1970s, developments which were to be responsible for so much growth in Islamic financial services), translates *takaful* only as 'mutual agreement', with no mention as yet of the technical meaning of 'insurance'. It is, then, essentially a model of mutual provision, not a profit-making model. Of course, commercial operators are motivated by the desire to make profit from it, and it has not been that easy to develop a form of *takaful* which generates adequate profit without losing the essence of mutuality, which is what makes it different from conventional insurance.

Models of takaful

The basic theoretical difference between *takaful* and insurance is that rather than paying premiums to the insurance provider that are a pure loss to the policy holder if no claim is made, the *takaful* policy holder is a member of a mutual organisation who makes a donation or gift to it. These donations, in Arabic *tabarru*, are considered by scholars to avoid the suggestion of *gharar* in conventional premiums, which some Muslims perceive to be a form of gambling on the likelihood of the insured event taking place. Any surplus left in the funds after claims and operating costs is distributed to the members. The difficulty in practice with this 'ideal type' model of pure mutuality is that it can only generate sufficient funds to meet all possible claims if organised on a very large scale. Even the global *takaful* industry would struggle to be viable if run on a purely mutual basis, and a *takaful* company serving only the British Muslim market would have no chance of being able to meet all claims reliably on this basis.

In practice, therefore, the mutual model is modified in one of several possible ways. The first is based on the fact that the theory of *takaful* allows for a manager to be employed to manage the fund on behalf of the members, and to be paid a fee for this out of the fund. This has been developed into a full-scale agency or *wakala* model, where the company that provides the service is conceived as the agent (*wakeel*) of the members and the agency fee constitutes its profit. In a strict *wakala* model it receives only a fixed fee, but supervising *shari'a* scholars have often ruled it acceptable for the agent to receive a share of the surplus funds also.

The other possibility is for the company to receive a share of the income generated by investing the pooled funds. This investment must, of course, itself be *shari'a* compliant, and a *mudaraba* model is favoured. One version of a *takaful* scheme allows the company operating it to receive only a share of the *mudaraba* investment income. The limited availability of compliant investment opportunities further restricts profitability, and this model has been described with some understatement as 'commercially challenging'.[1] More usually the operator will receive both a share of investment income and a share of the surplus left in the underwriting fund after meeting claims; even this though is often regarded as insufficient incentive by potential providers.

The most popular model is now a hybrid where the operator receives both a fixed fee, in accordance with the *wakala* model, and also a share of investment income as an incentive to manage the fund well. The practice departs further from the theory of pure mutuality in that, while as a matter of strict Islamic law it is the participants or policy holders who bear the underwriting risk, in order for a *takaful* fund to be viable in the reality of the modern world the operator, that is, the company that provides the coverage, has to indemnify the participants, that is, to guarantee to meet claims even if the donations of participants have not generated sufficient funds to do so. This contribution by the operator is conceptualised Islamically as a *qard hasan*, a philanthropic loan.

It will be seen that, while all the individual elements of *takaful* operations can be justified as *shari'a* compliant, the overall result is something quite a long way from the original attractive ideal of non-profit mutual reassurance and support. There are particular concerns about potential conflicts of interest between the participants and the operator, and about inadequate information being given to participants concerning the investment of contributions and distribution of surpluses.

The situation will probably improve as the *takaful* sector grows, introducing more choice and competition and making more funds available to reduce the risk of default. Some scholars believe that the institution of *waqf* offers exciting possibilities to develop *takaful*. The practice of

waqf has been an important part of Islamic culture for cen-
turies. It involves the donation of property to a charitable
purpose in perpetuity, with the income from the property
being used for the objects of the charity. The permanent
nature of the *waqf* donation gives a degree of security and
predictability that would be valuable in an insurance context. To date, though, the traditional institution of *waqf*
has not been employed by Muslim communities living in
countries where they are a religious minority. There would
be significant legal issues involved in introducing it in the
United Kingdom, but none of these should be insurmount-
able if the government continues to be supportive of Islamic
finance. The English legal institution of a charitable trust
approximates closely with the Islamic institution of *waqf*,
and therefore the latter could probably be incorporated
quite easily into the regulations which govern organisations
with charitable purposes. (Registered charities are super-
vised by the Charity Commission.) The difficulty would
arise from the addition of a profit-making element in the
takaful operation based on the *waqf*, which would prevent
the latter being treated simply as a charity.

The UK market

One early Bangladeshi writer[2] on the challenge of making
insurance acceptable to Muslims saw the UK scheme of
National Insurance as an exemplar of what Islamic insurance should be like. National Insurance is a compulsory
deduction from wages that gives entitlement to state benefits in unemployment, illness and retirement. This might
suggest that British Muslims would be particularly well
placed to develop the idea of non-profit-based social insurance, but there is little or no sign of National Insurance
providing inspiration for a new generation of British thinkers on Islamic finance. This is probably due to the fact that

National Insurance has now come to be seen simply as a payroll tax, and its link with the provision of particular benefits has been obscured. It is also, of course, the case that the development of *takaful* has been driven by commercial concerns, not social ones.

In the Muslim-majority world health insurance has been an important market for Islamic providers, but in the United Kingdom the availability of universal free health care, one of the benefits provided through the *takaful*-like system of National Insurance, means that the market for private health insurance is very small.

The UK market is seen as offering good opportunities for the development of an Islamic insurance industry primarily because motor vehicle insurance is compulsory. It differs from some other countries in that it is a legal requirement to insure one's car at least against claims by other drivers arising from accidents. The majority of drivers choose to insure against theft and damage by fire as well. Motor insurance was seen by the financial services industry as the initial market to enter with a *takaful* product. One newspaper[3] located a British Muslim man who kept his conscience clear on the subject of motor insurance by only ever keeping a car until the free insurance provided by the dealer had expired and then buying a new one with another term of free insurance. Such dedication might well inspire the insurance industry to believe that the *shari'a* compliant market could be a profitable one, though it must be doubted whether many Muslims would show such commitment.

The other obvious area for *takaful* product development is buildings insurance. This could be seen as a necessary corollary of Islamic house purchase finance. The provider has to have some protection against loss of the house, for example, due to destruction by fire, but for an Islamic lender to have to force their customers to take out *haraam* insurance is embarrassing. In the absence of *shari'a* compliant alternatives to conventional buildings insurance, the providers of Islamic home purchase plans have adopted a variety of ways of handling this problem. The IBB is the only UK provider that absolutely requires home buyers to take out buildings insurance themselves. This must be in the joint names of the bank and the buyer, with the bank named as first loss payee. The UNB 'recommends' that home buyers take out buildings insurance themselves, but says that it understands that some Muslims may not want to deal with insurance companies, and is prepared in this case to take out the policy itself, in its own name, and charge the customer for it. Bristol & West, the former supplier of Islamic home finance to Lloyds TSB, always took out buildings insurance in its own name and passed on the costs to the home buyer. Ahli Bank, in its Manzil plans, always arranges buildings insurance itself in the case of an *ijara* contract and includes the cost in the rental payments. With a *murabaha* contract it gives clients the option of arranging insurance themselves. HSBC Amanah offers customers the choice of arranging insurance themselves, but will also take out the policy itself and add the premiums to the customers' monthly payments. The version of the Amanah UK home finance information booklet currently available online states that the bank offers a *shari'a* compliant form of buildings insurance, home *takaful*. In fact, this is not available at present (see below), but this piece of marketing material illustrates the potential synergy of these two financial products. In theory, therefore, the home *takaful* market should grow in line with the growth in availability of Islamic house purchase products. Home contents insurance is also considered desirable by most householders, but since it is not obligatory, it is not a driver of the market in the same way as buildings and motor insurance.

The third main type of *takaful* product is the Islamic version of what in conventional finance is known as life insurance. In its Islamic form this is called family *takaful*. There have always been some doubts about whether a type of insurance that could be seen as speculating on the time of one's death is religiously acceptable. Calling it family *takaful* shifts the emphasis away from this aspect of the product and places it on the provision made for the long-term security of one's family, which is entirely laudable. The demographic profile of the British Muslim population shows a high proportion of young families, who are the most likely customers for this type of service, and makes this market an attractive one for the industry. In addition, the growth in the market for this type of *takaful* is also linked to the development of house purchase finance, because the buyer usually wishes to ensure that arrangements are in place to cover continued payments and enable the family to remain in their home in the event of his or her death or serious illness.

An uncertain start

Sadly, the optimism surrounding the development of a *takaful* industry in the United Kingdom has not been justified by the fortunes of the first two companies to enter the market. Coinciding as they did with the global banking crisis and severe economic recession, both failed in their first attempts. This does not reflect the true potential of the British market, and one hopes that in brighter economic times these two companies could still do well.

HSBC

HSBC, the large multinational bank, have well-established *takaful* services in the Muslim-majority world, so it was a relatively simple matter for them to extend the provision of a *takaful* product to the UK market. Home *takaful*, with policies available for both buildings and contents, was introduced in the United Kingdom in July 2005, but discontinued in December 2008.

HSBC used a modified *wakala* model. Part of the participants' contributions went to cover the agency fees and the rest was invested to provide income for the fund. The participants had first claim on the profits from investment and were paid an amount equivalent to 5 per cent of their contributions. The balance of the profit was divided equally between the participants and the company (the agent). If the profit should be insufficient to pay any more than this first claim of 5 per cent of contributions, all of it went to the participants and the company received nothing. If the profit was insufficient even to cover this amount, the participants received less than 5 per cent of their contributions or even nothing at all, having accepted the possibility of there being no profit to distribute as part of the conditions of their contract.

HSBC regarded its *takaful* policy as a 'premium' or 'gold standard' product, and reports that sales were 'modest'.[4] The bank never expected it to sell on the same scale as its Islamic home finance plans and current accounts, but it did believe that it was competitive with conventional insurance products aimed at the higher end of the market. The policy was supplied to HSBC by another company, Hamilton Insurance. The latter was sold to Norwich Union (later renamed Aviva) in 2008 and was no longer able to supply the *takaful* product to HSBC. This interesting and innovative product seems, therefore, to have been a victim both of the wave of changes in company ownership during 2008 and of the general contraction in demand for higher end products during the last few years. HSBC attempted to find another supplier, and at one stage entered into discussions with the independent *takaful* provider, Salaam Insurance (see below), but sadly was not able to reach agreement with any company. The bank intends to continue to review the situation. HSBC's information leaflets about its British Islamic services continued to include *takaful* for some time after it was no longer available, and the decision to discontinue it seems to have been one that HSBC was not anxious to publicise more than necessary, which suggests that they hope to reintroduce it at some stage.

Salaam

The first stand-alone *takaful* company in the United Kingdom was Salaam, launched in July 2008 after receiving approval from the FSA earlier in the year. Salaam Halaal Insurance is the brand name for the UK business of Principle Insurance Holdings, known previously as British Islamic Insurance Holdings, which was funded by large amounts of investment (reportedly £60 million) from several Muslim-majority countries, notably Saudi Arabia. This company was formed in 2005 and took several years to develop a model that satisfied the UK regulator.

It is noteworthy that the company chose not to use the word *takaful* in the brand name or marketing material of the British business, but rather to call it 'halaal insurance'. This suggests that their research had shown limited recognition of the Arabic word among their target market. Shortly after the launch, Principle's director of business development wrote an article for the leading British Muslim newspaper[5] in which he explained the working of *takaful* in detail, rather than assuming the readers were familiar with it. There is also, of course, the important matter that in the Internet age a company that avoids the word 'insurance' altogether in its marketing material will not be picked up in an online search by a potential customer who is not wholly committed to an Islamic product, but at that stage merely seeing what is available. This was particularly important to Salaam as the company was committed to direct selling by its website and by phone.

Salaam initially entered the market with only motor insurance, in line with the perception that this was the area that offered particularly good opportunities in the United Kingdom, but added home buildings and contents policies a year later. It planned eventually to add family *takaful* to its range, but never reached that point. By its own account of its structure, it employed a pure *wakala* model, that is, all operating costs and a satisfactory profit for the shareholders were covered by an agency fee alone and all profits from investment were added to the pooled donations fund. The surplus from the *tabarru* pool was distributed to policy holders in the form of a discount on their next year's payment. (This is quite distinct from the usual 'no claim' bonus.) The three members of the *shari'a* supervisory committee were Nizam Yaquby of Bahrain, Muhammad Elgari of Saudi Arabia and Abdul Barkatulla of the United Kingdom.

Salaam ceased to accept new customers in late 2009. At the time of writing it is still servicing existing policies, but these cannot be renewed. The launch of Salaam generated great excitement, so its closure caused correspondingly great disappointment. The company reported[6] that it had attracted about 10,000 customers, which was a creditable achievement, and there does not seem to have been anything intrinsically wrong with its business model. The problem was that it was not able to generate sufficient reserve funds to satisfy the requirements of the FSA. This difficulty in meeting capital reserve requirements is a recurrent theme in the story of Islamic finance in the United Kingdom. Salaam hoped to raise £80 million in a rights issue, but the results fell short by £20 million. With hindsight, the launch of Salaam was disastrously ill-timed, with the company's brief existence coinciding with a period of banking crisis, recession and high fuel prices. In fact, this period saw a fall in the number of cars on the roads of Britain for the first time ever, which was bad news for a provider of an alternative form of motoring insurance.

An especially interesting aspect of Salaam's original marketing was that the company claimed to be not only *shari'a* compliant, but able to offer cheaper premiums than the conventional competition. It seems obvious enough that an insurance company that does genuinely redistribute some of its profits to its customers will be more attractive than one that retains all its profits in the conventional manner; attractive to everyone, regardless of religious conviction. There must though be some doubt about how far a commercial concern will be able or willing to maintain a level of profit redistribution that would make its rates truly competitive with the conventional competition. It is unfortunate that Salaam did not survive long enough to test this model properly. A future *takaful* provider that attracted substantial interest from non-Muslims could potentially revolutionise the insurance industry.

Future prospects

Lloyd's of London is reported[7] to be interested in entering the *takaful* market. It is not likely to offer retail products to the general public, but would be focused on the secondary insurance and commercial markets. The lack of availability of re-*takaful* (a term, incidentally, which provides a striking example of the linguistic phenomenon known as 'Islamic English') is the most important factor hindering the growth of the Islamic insurance sector, so the entry of such a major player into the market would give the development of *takaful* a substantial boost. The main problem with the provision of a secondary market to insure the insurers, as it were, in the Islamic sector is the need to ensure strict separation of *shari'a* compliant funds from those that are non-compliant. The scale of funding needed is not easy to find from entirely compliant sources. Lloyd's apparently believes that the syndicate structure of its operations, with particular pools of funds dedicated to particular purposes, is well suited to ensuring this separation.

The authors of the article cited above are members of the Norton Rose team specialising in Islamic finance. Norton Rose is a law firm in the City of London with a specialist interest and expertise in Islamic financial services. It has taken a close interest in the development of *takaful*, since it expects to be the main provider of legal services to the UK *takaful* industry, and noted several years ago[8] that this problem of ensuring adequate financial reserves from compliant sources might cause some difficulty in satisfying the requirements of the FSA. In the aftermath of the banking crisis these requirements have become stricter and regulators more anxious.

The same study noted that there are some issues over the legal treatment of *takaful* since it is not strictly speaking insurance, but concluded that English law would treat a *takaful* contract in the same way as an insurance contract, because the difference between a premium and a donation was not significant. This is an example of the constant dilemma that Islamic financial practitioners face: in order to be competitive they must seek to be treated in the same way as conventional providers by the law and the regulators, while their appeal rests on maintaining that what they do is different in essence from conventional finance. This can sometimes seem like an endless attempt to square a circle.

Notes

1. Asaria, Iqbal, 'The spirit and model of takaful: meeting of minds or parting of ways?', *New Horizon*, July–September 2009.
2. Mannan, M. A. ([1975] 1986), *Islamic Economics: Theory and Practice*, London: Hodder & Stoughton.
3. 'Muslims torn between belief and finance', *The Observer*, 18 June 2000.
4. Personal communication dated 20 May 2010 from Amjid Ali, former Head of Amanah UK. Mr Ali also supplied details of the structure of the fund.
5. Gelu, Iqbal, 'Salaam halaal insurance', *Muslim News*, 29 August 2008.
6. These figures are taken from a report in *New Horizon*, January–March 2010.
7. Dingwall, Susan and Flockhart, Ffion, 'Lloyd's eyes on takaful', *Islamic Banking and Finance*, 7:4, August–September 2009.
8. Norton Rose (2003), *Takaful Insurance*. This paper is no longer available but a very similar paper dated December 2005 can be found at www.nortonrose.com.

CHAPTER 7
INVESTMENTS AND WEALTH MANAGEMENT

Having previously looked at savings accounts, where the depositor has no direct concern with how the funds are invested, this chapter will look at the wider field of investment, particularly direct investment in stocks and shares.

Screening of investments

There are a number of issues to consider when deciding whether an investment in the shares of a particular company is acceptable in Islam. The most obvious is the nature of the company's business. Directly prohibited in Islam are pork, alcohol and gambling, and the sexual morality of the religion is normally considered to preclude any form of pornography. Tobacco has not historically been specifically forbidden in Islam, but modern thinking is that it is precluded by the general prohibition of intoxicants as well as the deeper assumption that God desires us not to engage in behaviour that is harmful to us. Some scholars regard all forms of audio-visual entertainment as undesirable or even forbidden, because of a strict interpretation of traditions disapproving of music or acting or simply because it is seen as a waste of time that could be better spent in religious activities. The arms trade is usually regarded as unacceptable. While some individual Muslims might take the view that it depends rather on the intended destination of the arms, a fund manager cannot be expected to make political judgements of that nature, and a general ban aligns Islamic funds more closely with general 'ethical' ones. It goes without saying that all conventional financial services are forbidden.

Modern companies are so large and complex and have so many divisions involved in different areas of business that it has become very difficult to find companies that are absolutely free from any involvement in *haraam* activity. A consensus has arisen among scholars that a level of forbidden activity above 5 per cent makes a company unacceptable for investment. To take a simple example, a hotel or restaurant chain may well derive considerably more than 5 per cent of its profit from the sale of alcohol, and if so its shares are not a *shari'a* compliant investment, while an airline will probably be involved in supplying alcohol to its passengers, but this provides a negligible part of its income and so it is acceptable as an investment.

A more difficult form of screening concerns the Islamic prohibition of contractual uncertainty, speculation and practices so risky that they verge on gambling, which are all aspects of the complex concept of *gharar*. The general preference for trade over borrowing and funding through equity sales rather than debt financing has now solidified into the consensus opinion that a debt ratio of more than one third, or 33 per cent, makes a company non-compliant in *shari'a*. This ratio can be ascertained fairly easily from the company's accounts.

Intense debate has taken place in recent years over the acceptability of financial market innovations such as complex derivatives and hedge funds.[1] The details of this debate are outside the scope of this book. So far there is no Islamic hedge fund in the United Kingdom. It is a common complaint among writers on Islamic finance that there is no adequate way of managing risk in a *shari'a* compliant form. This rather seems to miss the point of the principle that any kind of increase of capital must come in return for a risk of loss. In the real world, investors do not want to have to face the possibility of loss. The question of exactly what degree of risk makes an investment *shari'a* compliant is therefore one that will probably never find a universally accepted answer.

Because so much analysis is required to determine whether a company is acceptable for a Muslim investor, the development of sophisticated software packages to carry out this task has been a prerequisite of the growth in Islamic equity investment. More recently, however, there have been some concerns that relying entirely on automation to screen companies may lead to error, because the description of the company's main area of business may disguise a subsidiary area that is unacceptable.[2] There is an additional cost involved in investigating companies thoroughly for *shari'a* compliance that may have to be passed on to the customer, but there is a reputational risk involved in not investigating them adequately.

Mutual funds

The first, and so far the only, Islamic mutual fund in the United Kingdom is the Islamic Global Equity Fund managed by Scottish Widows Investment Partnership (SWIP).[3] Scottish Widows is a company known primarily for pensions, but is also involved in general investment. It is now part of the Lloyds group but it is based in Edinburgh and, as the name suggests, has its origins in the provision of life insurance in Scotland. Long before it entered the Islamic sector it had adopted as its marketing image a picture of a woman wearing a long black cloak with a hood, who was presumably intended to look like a widow. This has proved fortuitously suitable for a company now targeting the Islamic market. The writer once witnessed a Scottish Widows promotion event in Canary Wharf, involving several women dressed in hooded black cloaks distributing company literature to passers-by, and was struck by how easily they blended with the women from the Gulf wearing black abayas who are fairly numerous in this London financial district.

The Islamic Global Equity Fund was set up in November 2005. The stated areas of exclusion from the fund are 'gambling, tobacco, the production or sale of pork products, the production of intoxicating liquor, non-Islamically structured banking, finance, investment or life insurance business, or any other interest-related activity, arms manufacturing and sectors/companies significantly affected by the above'. It invests only in companies that are listed in the Dow Jones Global Islamic Index and uses this index as a benchmark, but aims to outperform it by 2 per cent over three years.

So far, it seems to have fairly consistently outperformed the index by a small amount. Islamic funds generally have outperformed conventional funds over the last two years simply because they exclude shares in conventional financial services, which were plummeting over this period. To do better than the Islamic Index is more of a challenge. The main difference in regional allocation of funds between the SWIP fund and the Index is that the former has much less involvement in North America and much more in Europe, including the United Kingdom, and Japan. This presumably reflects an American bias in the Dow Jones organisation. In sector allocation the main differences are that SWIP has more involvement in 'industrials' and much less in 'basic materials'. SWIP also has slightly smaller allocation to consumer goods, health care, utilities, telecoms and oil and gas.

The overall impression is of less involvement in the main generators of wealth in the Gulf and other Muslim-majority countries and more focus on the fund's home region.

The *shari'a* advisory board for this fund consists of the familiar names of Nizam Yaquby, Imran Usmani, Abdul Barkatulla and Muhammad Nurullah Shikder.

Child Trust Funds

In an effort to encourage parents to invest for their children's future, the former Labour government introduced a scheme in which the parents of every baby in the country born after 1 September 2002 were sent a voucher for £250, which could only be invested in a Child Trust Fund (CTF). Babies of lower income parents received an additional £250. The fund could not be accessed by anybody except the named child on attaining the age of eighteen. Family and friends were permitted to make contributions to the fund of up to £1,200 per year, and the hope was that parents would get into the habit of making regular contributions. It was particularly hoped that families with no tradition of investing in the stock market could be familiarised with the practice by means of these children's funds.

This universal scheme created a dilemma for Muslim parents who were concerned that any investments they made should be *shari'a* compliant. The vouchers had an expiry date after which, if the parents had not chosen a fund provider, they would be invested by the government without further consultation. There was therefore some urgency about finding an acceptable fund before this happened. The compulsory element made the CTFs a more important driver of *shari'a* compliant investment provision than the small amount of money involved would suggest. The only *shari'a* compliant CTF is that provided by The Children's Mutual.[4] This is the only British investment company that specialises in financial provision for children, and it claims to manage one-third of all the country's Child Trust Funds. Representatives of British Muslim organisations approached this company soon after CTFs were introduced to discuss the creation of a compliant fund, without which parents would find their child's future being forcibly funded by non-compliant means. From the company's point of view, this is an almost entirely captive market. The Islamic fund is promoted under the name of the Shariah Baby Bond. All investments made by this fund are screened for *shari'a* compliance. The advisory board consists of the usual names of Nizam Yaquby, Imran Usmani, Abdul Barkatulla and Muhammad Nurullah Shikder.

The new government that came to power in May 2010 immediately announced the ending of the CTF scheme from January 2011. After that date no more government vouchers will be issued. Naturally, some parents will still wish to open trust funds for their children on their own initiative, but those who are not comfortable with invest-ment matters will no longer be obliged to think about them. Existing funds will continue in existence, and so the Shariah Baby Bond will continue to invest for the future of a sizeable cohort of British Muslim children.

Investment banks

There are now three banks in the City of London that under-take *shari'a* compliant asset management for institutions and wealthy individuals: the European Islamic Investment Bank (EIIB), Gatehouse Bank and the Bank of London and the Middle East (BLME). It can sometimes appear that the only British thing about these companies is that they are physically located in Britain. Even at a physical level they are keeping a low profile, being generally based on single floors of unobtrusive office buildings. Discretion is no doubt an important requirement of their clientele. A large proportion of both their investors and their investments are based overseas, notably in the Middle East. Some of their biggest funds are denominated in US dollars.[5] The reason for being based in London is the expertise available there and the favourable climate that the British government has created for Islamic banking. Many of the staff involved in Islamic banking in the City of London are themselves non-Muslim and are attracted to the sector simply by the perception that it is a growing sector that offers good career prospects and earning opportunities.

All these investment banks tailor their asset management advice to particular clients, creating a new fund for them if necessary. This makes it difficult to obtain information about their screening criteria. The EIIB's exclusions are alcohol, tobacco, pork, 'most' conventional financial services, 'much' of the defence sector and 'much' of the entertainment sector. A publication by the EIIB describes its investment approach as 'sector agnostic subject to sharia compliance'.[6] This is a fruitful phrase for initiating a debate on how far Islamic investment should exercise positive choice of sectors that it is considered desirable to promote rather than simply avoiding those that are forbidden.

The *shari'a* advisory board of the EIIB consists of Nizam Yaquby, Abdul Ghuddah and one name less frequently encountered, Abdul Latif Mahmood Al Mahmood of Bahrain. That of the BLME includes Imran Usmani and three names less well known in the United Kingdom: Mohammed Daud Baker, Esam Khalaf Al-Enezi and the chairman, Abdulaziz al-Qassar. Rather unusually, the bank has not included biographies of these scholars on its website.

Gatehouse Bank has a more interesting approach to religious oversight, in as much as it offers *shari'a* advisory services as one of its commercial activities. It will advise on the compliance of particular products and also provide general training in Islamic banking. The head of this advisory team is the prominent British scholar, Muhammad Nurullah Shikder. He is supported by another British scholar, Shahid Feroz, who was trained in religious scholarship at the Dar al-Uloom in Bury, Lancashire after studying secular law at Durham University. The third member of the team is Moilim el-Azar, who trained in Pakistan. It would be nice to think that the provision of training in Islamic finance by a predominantly British scholarly team could help to impart a more truly British character to a future generation of Islamic bankers.

Investment managers

Islamic equity funds worldwide are estimated to be worth US$16 billion,[7] but few of them are based in the United Kingdom, and even fewer are accessible to British Muslims who want to save regularly from a salary rather than invest large sums that they have inherited or gained in business. It is a sector with which many investment advisory companies are keen to become involved but there is little that is distinctively British about it.

The first serious attempt to help Muslim investors in the United Kingdom was the launch of the IslamiQ website in 2000. This was a commercial enterprise that provided advice and guidance on all aspects of Islamic finance, sold *shari'a* compliant investments and allowed the trading of approved shares online. It seems to have been a product of the general enthusiasm for Internet companies during this period and had ambitious plans for raising further capital, which were not realised. It is no longer in existence, but it served a useful purpose for a time.

A similar service was offered by iHilal Financial Services,

a subsidiary of Rasmala Investments (UK), which was set up in 2001. It aimed to identify and make accessible to Muslims based in the United Kingdom the best available Islamic financial products from whatever source. It continued in operation for a number of years, but now has apparently closed down.

HSBC Amanah introduced its Global Equity Fund to the United Kingdom in 2000. The minimum investment in this fund was US$25,000 and so it was promoted to Muslim business people rather than individual savers. This fund is no longer available in the same form; HSBC now offers a *shari'a* compliant investment fund only in the form of a pension (see below).

Parsoli launched its Global Islamic Equity Fund in 2001, and claimed it as the first UK-based *shari'a* compliant fund and the first Islamic fund to be approved by the FSA. Parsoli is an Indian investment management company that specialises in attracting British Muslims to invest in Indian Muslim companies. This fund seems to have become inactive and Parsoli no longer has a dedicated UK website. It is though still listed as having an office in Dewsbury, West Yorkshire. It took the unusual decision to locate its UK branch there, in the heart of a large Muslim community, rather than in London.

In August 2003, the Fyshe Group launched an Islamic stockbroking service under the name Fyshe Crestar (taking the name from the Muslim symbols of the crescent and star). It announced this as the first *shari'a* compliant service of its kind in the United Kingdom. The company acknowledged that compliant investment funds already existed, but argued that they were merely passive tracker funds, while Fyshe was offering an active advice and execution service for individual stocks and portfolio management. Press releases at the time of the launch laid stress on the fact that the restrictions on the areas in which Muslims could invest were causing them to be overexposed to certain sectors, notably property and information technology, and this was why Muslim investors needed more individually tailored advice. This service was launched, coincidentally or not, only a few weeks after the introduction of the HSBC Islamic home finance plan, and benefited from the resulting media attentiveness to Islamic finance. Unfortunately, Fyshe Crestar appears now to have been inactive for some time, although there has been no formal announcement of its closure.

Pensions

Fyshe Crestar announced the introduction of a *shari'a* compliant pension in 2004 and promoted it as the first such pension in the United Kingdom. Its current status is uncertain, but it is no longer being actively marketed. Around this period several other companies announced that they would be introducing *shari'a* compliant pensions, but none of this excitement seems to have resulted in anything concrete. The interest in Islamic pensions at this period was due to the introduction at the end of 2003 of a legal directive[8] forbidding discrimination in employment on the grounds of religion (as opposed to race), which could potentially be interpreted as applying to a situation where Muslim employees were disadvantaged by the lack of a pension scheme that conformed with their religious beliefs. It seems that a number of investment companies are still interested in entering the Islamic pensions sector, if they could do so without disproportionate expense. As the British Muslim population increases and ages this will be a growth area and probably one that will reward early entry.

At the time of writing, the only active provider of a *shari'a* compliant pension in the United Kingdom is HSBC. Amanah UK offers an Islamic investment fund that is now available only as a pension.[9] The Amanah Global Equity Index Fund can be invested in only through the HSBC Life Amanah Pension Fund. This fund was launched in April 2004. It is a passive tracker fund that takes the Dow Jones Islamic Titans 100 Index as its benchmark. Its latest performance statement (March 2010) appears to indicate that it has underperformed this benchmark slightly over the lifetime of the fund.

The *shari'a* supervisors of this fund are those on the central committee of HSBC, who have been listed elsewhere. The stated exclusions from the fund are alcohol, tobacco, gambling, pornography, pork, weapons, conventional financial services and leisure and media. The exclusion of all forms of media places it at the more restrictive end of the scale, but presumably this reflects the provisions of the Dow Jones. The exact wording is that companies whose 'primary activity' is in these sectors are excluded. There is no mention of excluding a company if it derives more than 5 per cent of its income from them. In addition, companies must have a proportion of debt, cash and interest bearing securities and accounts receivable of less than 33 per cent of twelve-month trailing market capitalisation.

The bank explains that since it is impossible to completely exclude some level of *haraam* business activity among the companies included, the proportion of income derived from non-compliant sources is 'purified' by being donated to charity. In fact, it is given to the bank's own charity, the HSBC in the Community Middle East Foundation. Evidently, it has not seemed worthwhile to the bank to establish a British version of this charitable community activity.

1st Ethical

1st Ethical is a company founded in Bolton, Lancashire in 2001 by Sufyan Ismail, a second generation British

Muslim who studied economics and corporate finance at Manchester University and then worked in conventional finance for three years before qualifying as an independent financial adviser and setting up his own company. It was always made quite clear that this was a company dedicated to Islamic finance, but it adopted a policy of welcoming non-Muslims both as clients and as staff. The decision to use the word 'ethical' in the name rather than anything explicitly Islamic both reflects this openness and makes a strong statement of belief that Islamic finance is identical with ethical finance.

1st Ethical originally specialised in independent financial advice and tax planning. Its website in its first few years stated that it specialised in the 'mitigation of tax through the use of Inland Revenue sanctioned, Shariah compliant trusts', which neatly expresses the way the *shari'a* has become part of the regulatory framework in which some finance professionals work. The use of the word 'compliance' to refer to religious acceptability has now become so routine as to be unremarked, but it is perhaps worth reflecting on the historical process by which a word whose real referent is the Islamic 'path' of divinely approved behaviour has come to be routinely bracketed with the tax collection department of the United Kingdom.

1st Ethical has now ceased to exist as a company, but has become the name of a charitable trust set up as part of OneE Group, the larger entity into which the original 1st Ethical has now developed. In 2007 OneE decided to discontinue its investment advisory work and concentrate entirely on tax planning and venture capital activities. The latter is described in Chapter 9. Tax planning apparently proved to be the most lucrative area of the company's original activities, because the economic polarisation of the British Muslim population, noted in Chapter 1 of this book, has produced a disproportionate number of clients liable to higher rates of tax. The tax advisory company was set up in 2007 and is called OneE Tax. It has chosen not to mention anything in its publicity about the fact that it is run on Islamic principles, but to position itself as a mainstream advisory service.

Both the original 1st Ethical and now OneE Tax have won numerous industry awards, particularly for entrepreneurship. The company and its founder have always shown a flair for publicity and have received a great deal of positive coverage in both the business and the general press. The whole history of the company is an admirable example of a business enterprise that has used the mainstream opportunities available in Britain (higher education and grants for new businesses) to create an Islamic service and found that it can be very successful commercially by so doing. It is almost the story of British Islam in microcosm, particularly in the way it disproves the assumption of the early commentators on migrant communities that economic advancement and social integration would be achieved only by wholesale and uncritical adoption of the culture of the host society.

What makes OneE more than just a successful company is the fact that it has devoted as much effort to the general promotion of Islamic finance as to its own commercial activities. From the early days of 1st Ethical it produced numerous booklets and 'research papers' aimed at educating British Muslims about their heritage in this area and sent its staff out to give talks in mosques, in schools, on local radio or anywhere else it could secure an invitation. This educational activity has now been formally hived off as 1st Ethical Charitable Trust. The trust is also involved in development aid work among Muslim communities overseas. It is registered with the Charity Commission, which regulates British charities, so apparently the religious education aspect of its work is not considered incompatible with charitable status. It is stated that this trust is funded entirely by the commercial activities of OneE and is not dependent on outside donations. If this is indeed so then it is an impressive example of using the fees extracted from the targeted 'high net worth clients' in gratitude for the 'bespoke tax mitigation strategies' provided to fund community activity among British Muslims. One could wish that more of the wealth found in the world of Islamic banking were redistributed in this way.

The trust's stated aim is 'to empower British Muslims with the knowledge required to conduct their legal and financial affairs in a shariah compliant manner'.[10] One of the booklets and many of the lectures have the catchy title *Make Yourself Shariah Compliant*, and the booklet provides a useful list of providers of Islamic financial products in the United Kingdom. The production of literature on Islamic finance has increased and has recently culminated in a book, described with typical brio as 'the UK's first ever comprehensive text book on Islamic finance'.[11] Staff continue to give talks to any interested organisation, including universities, and the educational effort has now embraced video and is available in the form of 'webtorials'.

Potentially the most significant aspect of all this effort at raising awareness of and knowledge about Islamic finance is that 1st Ethical has created its own group of *shari'a* scholars to produce its educational literature and to provide advice free of charge to anyone who wants it on 'contemporary legal and financial issues'.[12] This organisation is called Al-Qalam ('the pen', the title of a *sura* of the Quran) and it is described as independent from 1st Ethical, although apparently funded by it. The five scholars who contribute to it are all British – 'a home grown panel' – and stand out in sharp distinction from the handful of familiar names who advise all of the banks. The only member of this panel who also advises large banks is Abdul Qadir Barkatulla. The panel is chaired by Zubair Butt, who trained in Pakistan but also in Dewsbury, and now holds a position at an Islamic college in Bradford. He is therefore a representative product of the Muslim community of West Yorkshire. The vice-chair is Haitham Tamim, who previously worked in Lebanon. Mohammed Ibn Adam trained in Bury, Lancashire as well as in Pakistan and Syria and now lives in Leicester, home of a very large Muslim community. Yusuf Sacha trained in India and is now a lecturer at the Islamic college in Dewsbury. This group of people collectively embodies the real British Muslim experience.

Part of their work is the provision of *khutba* (sermon) material to mosques. It was noted in the introductory chapter of this book that there is a widespread perception that imams who came to Britain from abroad are not always well equipped to offer advice on contemporary financial matters. The identification of this medium of education and, arguably, marketing, is astute. 1st Ethical could be said to have worked on creating its own market through this intensive effort to spread knowledge of Islamic finance. The way in which its activities subsequently developed demonstrate that this would be too cynical an interpretation. But the long-term result of this educational activity could be to entrench a demand for Islamic financial products and inspire future entrepreneurs to supply it.

Wills

The emergence of a need for guidance on how to transmit wealth to the next generation marks, at one level, the ageing of the British Muslim population, as the first generation of migrants pass away, but at a deeper level it is a sign of the permanence and stability of the community. The making of a will to govern the disposition of one's assets after death is a form of wealth management, and is a duty always urged on clients by financial advisers.

The founder of 1st Ethical, Sufyan Ismail, who is a qualified financial adviser, has championed the cause of Islamic wills from the early days of the company. In his dealings with Muslim clients he had found a worrying lack of awareness of what would happen to their assets after their death if they did not make explicit provision for this. Some clients had refused to make a will because they wished to follow Islamic inheritance rules and rejected the provisions of English law on the subject. They believed erroneously that if they did not make a conventional will then the law of England would not apply and their family would be free to deal with the estate in a way that conformed with *shari'a*. Mr Ismail devoted considerable effort to explaining the concept of intestacy to such clients, to make them understand that if they should die without a will then the default provisions of English law would be applied without any reference to their wishes as expressed during life. One of his clients actually told him that he was not sure if making a will was permissible in Islam, which he found particularly upsetting because 'alhamdolillah, the brother is one of the wealthiest businessmen in the area'.[13] On the contrary, making a will is, the company stresses, 'a neglected sunnah', and all of its literature on estate planning includes the relevant *hadith*. 'It is a duty of a Muslim who has anything to bequeath not to let two nights pass without including it in his Will' (recorded by al-Bukhari).

The work of 1st Ethical on incorporating Islamic inheritance laws into a will that is valid in English law has now culminated in the production of a will template, approved by the Al-Qalam panel of *shari'a* scholars, which is available free of charge from the company website.[14] The company hopes that downloaders of the template, particularly those whose assets will be liable for inheritance tax, will then decide to pay for its advice on how to minimise taxation of their estate.

Islamic law specifies the proportions of an estate that should be awarded to each surviving relative. Because it is not possible to know for certain in advance which relatives will survive the testator, the company advises setting up a trust in the will that is authorised to distribute assets according to these Islamic prescriptions. It is the setting up of the trust that must be valid in English law. The standard will begins with a statement of faith and a wish that Muslim burial practice should be followed. It then appoints executors and trustees in the normal manner, and proceeds to instruct that the estate is 'absolutely to be distributed and where relevant invested in accordance with Shariah (Islamic Law), the interpretation and application of which my Trustees in their absolute discretion shall determine provided that such distribution does not breach English Law in which case my Trustees shall apply such modifications as are necessary to comply with English Law'.

The main difference between Islamic custom and the default position of English law is that the former awards the bulk of the estate to the children of the deceased, rather than giving everything to a surviving spouse. The most likely reason for a conflict to arise between Islamic and English law is that the former awards smaller shares in the estate to female children than to male. A daughter who chose to challenge her smaller share of the estate in a secular court would probably win. The wording of the will would appear to place a heavy burden of interpretation on the trustees, and it would be almost essential for one of them to be a Muslim solicitor. Islamic probate is surely a niche area of legal practice that will offer increasing professional opportunities as the Muslim community grows and hopefully becomes more affluent. This is, however, outside the scope of this book.

The aspect of Islamic probate which is relevant to a study of Islamic investment practice is that it is normally a legal requirement that executors and trustees obtain the highest possible price for all estate assets sold and the highest rate of interest on funds invested during the probate process. Executors who placed the funds in their charge in a deposit account that does not pay interest would normally be considered to be negligent and liable to be sued by the heirs. The final two clauses of this Islamic will template state that the trustees 'are requested to have regard to generally accepted Islamic principles of investment and shall not be liable for the consequences of following such principles, nor for any loss to the Trust Fund that may result from investing, or keeping the Trust Fund or any part of it invested, in Islamic investments rather than non-Islamic investments', and furthermore that they 'shall not be obliged to insure any part of the Trust Fund and shall not be liable for the consequences of not insuring any part of the Trust Fund'.

It is also normally the case that registered charities are required to earn the maximum return on their invested donations, but the Charity Commission has stated that it will not oblige an Islamic charity to invest its funds in interest-bearing accounts, because it accepts that the observation of Islamic principles is part of the charity's essential purpose.[15] No doubt the 1st Ethical Charitable Trust has taken advantage of this acknowledgement.

Notes

1. See the following *Financial Times* articles: 'Path opens for Islamic finance hedging', 1 March 2010; 'Hedge funds: indus-

try once more at centre of attention', 12 May 2010; 'Derivatives "in need of robust architecture"', 12 May 2010.

2. Donia, Mohamed and Marzban, Shehab, 'Patching holes in the net', *Islamic Banking and Finance*, October–November 2008.

3. www.swip.com. The information cited was supplied by Scottish Widows' media centre. A detailed case study of this fund can be found in Schoon, Natalie (2011), *Islamic Asset Management: An Asset Class on its Own?* Edinburgh: Edinburgh University Press.

4. www.thechildrensmutual.co.uk. Search for Shariah Baby Bond.

5. A case study of the BLME's US dollar fund can be found in Schoon (2011).

6. 'Private equity and corporate advisory', European Islamic Investment Bank, January 2010, available at www.eiib.co.uk.

7. *The Financial Times*, 2 July 2009.

8. The Employment Equality (Religion or Belief) (Amendment) Regulations 2003.

9. www.assetmanagement.hsbc.com/uk/amanah.

10. www.1stethical.com, accessed 3 June 2010.

11. El-Diwany, Tarek (ed.) (2010), *Islamic Banking and Finance: What It Is and What It Could Be*, Bolton: 1st Ethical Charitable Trust. The quotation is from the 1st Ethical newsletter for Winter 2008. (Characteristically, they were publicising the book well in advance.)

12. This information is taken from www.alqalam.org.uk and www.1stethical.com/charitable-trust, accessed 4 June 2010.

13. Ismail, Sufyan, *Preparing an Islamic inheritance strategy in light of the inheritance taxation laws of England and Wales*, p. 2. This is an undated paper produced during the early years of the company's work on estate planning that is no longer available. The company's current publication on the subject is: 1st Ethical Charitable Trust, *Preparing an Islamic Will*, 2nd edn 2008.

14. www.1stethical.com. The will template is prominently adver-
    tised on the home page.
15. Personal communication from Debbie Nunn of the Charity
    Commission dated 1 February 2005.

The word *sukuk* is the plural form of *sakk*, which means a written note of a financial transaction. It is usually translated as 'Islamic bonds', but *sukuk* are not the same as conventional bonds. Their development as an Islamic asset class originated in a decision promulgated in 1988 by the Fiqh Academy of the Organisation of the Islamic Conference that any collection of assets can be represented in a written note and that this note can be traded, as long as it represents mostly physical assets, rather than cash or debt. One of the principles that Islamic finance must observe is that debt cannot be traded.

With a conventional bond, money is lent to a company or government by an investor in return for the payment of a fixed rate of interest. This fixed interest naturally makes them unacceptable to an observant Muslim investor. In the Islamic alternative a return is paid to the investor from the income stream generated by an underlying asset, usually some kind of property. All the different kinds of *halaal* forms of income generation can be used in *sukuk*. Indeed, the Accounting and Auditing Organisation for Islamic Financial Institutions (AAOIFI) has described fourteen different kinds of structure for *sukuk*. Some types of contract are considered by scholars to be acceptable ways to generate income, but not acceptable for trading in a second-ary market. This applies particularly to *murabaha* and *bay'* *salam* contracts, which are only permissible if the original contracting parties complete the terms of the contract, that is, repay the money, themselves. To transfer entitlement to the repayments under a *murabaha* contract would be too similar to trading in debt. With *mudaraba* and *mush-araka* based *sukuk*, that is, where the return is generated from trading activity undertaken by the issuer, the capital invested cannot be guaranteed, and if taken seriously this lack of guarantee is a deterrent to investors.

The consultation process

In 2006 the British government, having already introduced a number of legislative and regulatory changes that encour-aged the development of Islamic financial services, began to express an interest in issuing *sukuk*. In April 2007, the Islamic Finance Experts Group was set up to begin formal consideration of this possibility, and in November 2007 the Treasury published a report on the results of this considera-tion and invited responses from interested and knowledge-able parties.[1] The conclusions of the consultation process were published in the form of a new report in June 2008.[2] Another consultation process was later undertaken to gauge opinion on the introduction of certain specific legislative changes that would make the regulatory treatment of *sukuk* more similar to that of the conventional instruments whose functions they were designed to replicate. The conclusions of this consultation were published jointly by the Treasury and the Financial Services Authority in October 2009.[3] During this period the Treasury also produced a general review of government policy towards Islamic finance, which was published in December 2008.[4]

The progress of this preparatory programme of consultation and legislative amendment was generally known and followed in the world of Islamic banking, not just in the United Kingdom but internationally. The prospect of a British government issuance of *sukuk* was eagerly antici- pated and, more than once, was reported to be imminent.[5] To date, however, no actual issuance has taken place. In November 2008, the government announced that it had decided not to proceed with *sukuk* issuance for the time being, giving as the reason that it 'would not offer value for money'. The fact that the Treasury and the FSA continued to study the legislative aspects of *sukuk* issuance in the year following this announcement implies that the government had not permanently renounced the idea, but merely post- poned it. There are a number of probable reasons for this. First, and most obviously, the general seizure in the world's financial markets from 2008 onwards made the time inaus- picious to launch a new asset class already regarded by some as dangerously novel. By the time the markets began to look more promising the government was near the end of its term in office and knew that it would probably lose the gen- eral election, so any issuance had become a matter for its successor. In addition, there were worries over some aspects of the religious approval and secular regulation of *sukuk* that persisted throughout the consultation process.

Why do it?

It was made clear that the motivation for issuing *sukuk* was a dual one: to attract investment from overseas, particularly the Middle East, into Britain, and to improve the range of religiously acceptable financial products available to British Muslims. This was set out quite explicitly at the opening of the consultation document, in the form of a quotation from the then Economic Secretary to the Treasury, Ed Balls: 'We are determined to do everything we can to deliver greater opportunities for British Muslims – and also to entrench London as a leading centre for Islamic finance in the world.'

There is a certain amount of scepticism in Britain about the extent to which the government, in its introduction of measures to support Islamic finance, has really been concerned to help its Muslim citizens rather than to attract Islamic investment from overseas into the country, and so it is noteworthy that when a definite conflict arose between these two aspirations in the process of planning for *sukuk* issuance, the decision came down on the side of helping British Muslims even if it might be at the cost of losing some overseas investment. Some respondents to the consultation felt strongly that the *sukuk* issuance should be denominated in US dollars and that denomination in sterling would reduce its attractiveness to overseas investors. The Treasury acknowledged the validity of this point, but stated that the issuance would be in sterling because this would 'better meet its objectives'. Some observers believed that there was never any serious possibility that it would be denominated in dollars because that would involve a foreign exchange risk to the Treasury. The report though makes no mention of this point, but states that sterling issuance would 'facilitate the provision of Sharia'a compliant retail products in the UK, secure the potential benefits to domestic Islamic banks and facilitate ease of structuring'.[6]

It was felt that one area of Islamic financial services that would particularly benefit from the availability of sovereign *sukuk* would be the *takaful* industry. It would make it much easier for *takaful* companies to manage their funds efficiently, and be sure of being able to meet claims, if they could keep some of their cash reserves in *sukuk* and have confidence in being able to liquidate them when necessary. The main problem in the development of *takaful* has been the shortage of *shari'a* compliant short-term investments. This has also been an obstacle to the development of retail deposit accounts in the Islamic sector. Banks have been obliged to rely heavily on commodity *murabaha* and *tawarruq* to generate a *halaal* return on the cash deposited. Some scholars are unhappy about this, and it is also unsatisfactory in banking terms because there are high fixed costs associated with commodity trading. The Treasury hoped that the availability of short-term *sukuk* would make it possible to offer retail savings accounts where the return of the capital could be guaranteed, which, of course, it cannot be in a profit-and-loss-sharing account based on commodity trading. It seems doubtful though that such capital guaranteed products would ever meet with general scholarly approval.

In a related consultation exercise, National Savings and Investment, an organisation linked to the Treasury that offers retail savings products, studied the possibility of adding an Islamic savings account to their range.[7] It was intended that NS&I would be the first to introduce the new forms of retail Islamic financial services that would be enabled by a government issuance of *sukuk*. This review concluded that the viability of an Islamic investment product would be dependent on being able to market it to the 'ethical' customer as well as to Muslims, and believed that the best way of doing this would be to choose something with a strong environmental image as the underlying asset of the *sukuk*. The preferred 'physical ethical asset' was a wind farm or solar power array. While this innovative idea has not yet been realised in practice, it is hard to believe that it will be permanently abandoned because, once encountered, the image of wind farm based *sukuk* is difficult to forget. Something like it could well come into existence in the future when economic conditions are more favourable.

The Treasury consultation considered in detail the relative advantages and drawbacks of what they referred to as 'bond like' and 'bill like' *sukuk*. This wording was carefully chosen to avoid giving the impression that Islamic investment certificates were no different in their essential nature from conventional interest-bearing bonds and bills. The difference between bonds and bills with which they were concerned is the length of the term before maturity. *Sukuk* with terms of one year or more were classed as 'bond like' and those with terms of less than a year as 'bill like'. Because the main perceived lack in the Islamic banking sector is means of short-term liquidity management, the conclusions report came down on the side of a 'bill like' issuance as being the priority. It was hoped that a secondary market in trading *sukuk* would develop over time as the result of successive issuances of government *sukuk*. An additional advantage of this was thought to be that the pricing of *sukuk* might become an alternative 'benchmark' for the pricing of other forms of Islamic financial products, a more truly Islamic one that could replace the reliance on the LIBOR and Bank of England base rates of interest.

Structure

Only two possible structures for a government *sukuk* were seriously considered: *ijara* and *mudaraba*. Any excessively complex structures were felt to be undesirable both in terms of the costs of setting them up and the possibility that they might be judged not to be fully *shari'a* compliant.

Internationally, 80 per cent of *sukuk* are based on *ijara* structures,[8] and this was always the clear preference for a government issuance. The structure finally chosen was one that the Treasury insisted on referring to throughout the consultation process as 'a plain vanilla *ijara*', a regrettable example of the infelicities that can result when 'Islamic

English' meets up with the colloquialisms of the financial markets. What was meant was a straightforward leasing contract with no complicating factors.

A government-owned property is transferred into a special purpose vehicle (SPV). The SPV issues *sukuk* certificates to investors that give a share in the 'usufruct' of the property, that is, the income arising from it in the form of rent. The rents constitute the profit on the investment in place of an interest payment on a conventional bond or bill, and are paid to the certificate holders periodically. At the end of the term the SPV redeems the certificates and gives the investors their money back. All of the problematic parts of this arrangement concern the transfer of the asset. The SPV buys the head lease of the property from the government and then the government sub-leases it back. The government pays rent to the SPV for this sub-lease, which the SPV then pays out to the investors. At the end of the term of the *sukuk* the government buys back the head lease from the SPV. A promise is given that it will do this at the outset of the arrangement. A unilateral promise of this kind is acceptable in *shari'a*, whereas a bilateral contract would not be, because contracts which are dependent on other contracts are regarded as impermissible in Islamic law, being a form of *gharar* or uncertainty. Some scholars, however, are unhappy about the increasing use of unilateral promises as a way of getting around the ban on interdependent contracts. The fact that the property on which the *sukuk* is based has to be transferred back and forth in this way creates multiple liability for stamp duty land tax, and possibly various other taxes, such as value added tax (VAT). This produced grumbling among some commentators, who felt that the legislative effort needed to go even further to equalise treatment of *sukuk* and conventional debt instruments.[9] One could question whether an exemption from stamp duty can be granted without rendering the asset transfer synthetic (a question that arguably also arises in the case of the exemption from stamp duty granted for Islamic home purchase finance). Some less sympathetic observers already take the view that there is no real transfer of ownership involved in the creation of a SPV.[10]

An alternative structure for the *sukuk* issuance, which was ultimately rejected, was that of *mudaraba*. In this the SPV becomes the *rab al-maal* (the entity in charge of the money) and the government becomes the *mudarib* (the entrepreneur). The SPV gives the proceeds of the issuance of certificates to the government and, in its capacity as *mudarib*, the government invests the money in some profit-generating *shari'a* compliant project that generates the returns periodically paid to the certificate holders. In this structure the government also gives a unilateral promise to buy back the assets from the SPV, in the same way as it does in the case of an *ijara* structure. Strictly speaking, in a *mudaraba* or *musharaka* structure the investors' capital cannot be guaranteed, because the return comes in the form of a profit on trade that is not certain. In the event, during the period between the publication of the Treasury's consultation document in which these alternative structures were outlined, and the appearance of the conclusions of the consultation process, the *sukuk* industry was shaken by an announcement of scholarly disapproval of this element of *sukuk* structuring.

The impact of the Usmani statement

Muhammad Taqi Usmani, the Pakistani judge and scholar who has been a very prominent figure in the development of Islamic banking worldwide, serves as the chairman of the *shari'a* board of AAOIFI. In this capacity he issued a statement towards the end of 2007 in which he expressed concerns about the *shari'a* compliance of some current *sukuk* issuances. In February 2008, this was expanded into a statement by AAOIFI on the essential characteristics of *sukuk*. Mufti Usmani felt that there was no real sharing of risk involved in the structure of some of the most common kinds of *sukuk*, and that they were therefore not truly in accordance with the spirit of *shari'a*. This was generally reported in a simplified version in which he had said that '85% of *sukuk* do not comply with *shari'a*'. *Sukuk* issuance internationally dropped sharply in 2008, although this was also related to the wider problems in the financial markets during that year.

It seems that it was particularly the promise to buy back assets from the SPV in *mudaraba* or *musharaka* structures of *sukuk* that was problematic, because if the promise is to buy them back at the same price and not at the current market value then this means in effect that the investors' capital is guaranteed. The AAOIFI scholars felt that the trend was towards this type of *sukuk* and that it was the effective guarantee that was making it attractive. They responded by urging the Islamic banking industry to return to the fundamental *shari'a* principles of sharing risk and reward. This is part of a wider pattern in Islamic financial services, that the practice continually drifts away from risk sharing and towards guaranteed returns, while the supervising scholars periodically drag it back.

When the response to the consultation on *sukuk* issuance by the British government was published in June 2008, with the impact of Mufti Usmani's statement still fresh in the minds of all concerned, the conclusion had been reached that an *ijara* structure was a safer option as it had wider scholarly acceptability and there were no *shari'a* objections to buying back the underlying assets at face value or to trading the *sukuk* certificates.

The impact of defaults

The use of a *sukuk* to finance its purchase of the Aston Martin car manufacturer by Investment Dar, a Kuwaiti company, helped to raise the profile of this form of financing (because it gave journalists an excuse to print pictures of expensive cars), and so when in May 2009 the company defaulted on repayment this was also prominently reported. In the next few months two other large companies defaulted on *sukuk* payments. This prompted the holders of the investment certificates to seek recourse to the underlying assets of the *sukuk*, which are in theory the security that makes *sukuk* safer than conventional bonds. The situation then became even more worrying for investors, when in December 2009 Nakheel, the company responsible for some of the largest building projects in Dubai, announced that it was seeking to reschedule its repayment of a US$4 billion *sukuk*. In the event, default was narrowly avoided when the company was given financial assistance by Abu Dhabi, and it is clear that the economic difficulties that brought about this particular crisis were peculiar to Dubai. However, the legal uncertainty that was exposed by the threat of default has had an important impact on the development of *sukuk* internationally.

Preliminary comments by those familiar with the industry indicated that the assumption that the investors had a real claim on the underlying assets might well be mistaken.[11] All the contracts in question were made under English law, and so the United Kingdom would be directly concerned in any resulting court case. While a definitive court verdict has not yet been given, it is the opinion of most commentators that in English law the certificate holders have only a beneficial right to the asset, that is, to receive its rents or profits, not a legal title to the asset itself. Therefore, they are not entitled to insist in the case of default that the property on which the *sukuk* is based is sold and the proceeds divided among the certificate holders. This is a fundamental challenge to the claim of the supporters of *sukuk* that it is a safer and more honest type of investment product than conventional bonds, because it is supported by real assets and not by intangible debt. Until this dispute over the interpretation of the structure of *sukuk* is resolved the issuance of *sukuk* is bound to slow down. It will have a particular impact on the prospect of a British government issuance, because the British government cannot be seen to be promoting an Islamic investment by employing claims about the rights of investors that have been found to be unreliable by an English court.

The political issues

Naturally any decisions taken by government have a political dimension, even if the debate is couched in purely economic terms, and in considering a sovereign *sukuk* issuance the British Government is treading a rather fine political line.

All political parties in Britain seek to attract the Muslim vote. During their period in opposition the Conservative Party actively courted the Muslim community, regularly sending party leaders along to Eid celebrations and the like on the premises of Muslim organisations. Historically, all communities of migrant origin have voted overwhelmingly for the Labour Party, partly because they believed it to be more accepting of racial and religious difference and partly because the first generation of immigrants mostly belonged to occupational groupings whose indigenous members also voted overwhelmingly for Labour. As the population of migrant origin has become established and subsequent generations have become more diversified in their occupational and income profiles, this affiliation has begun to weaken. The Iraq war of 2003 caused a dramatic, and apparently permanent, drop in the level of support for the Labour government of the day among Muslims. Rival parties saw a community of floating voters whose support was there for the winning. The Conservative Party, in particular, believed that the successful business people who formed a larger than average proportion of the British Muslim population were natural Conservative voters and just needed to be made aware of the fact. The Labour Party in power, meanwhile, was conscious that it had a lot of ground to make up with its Muslim citizens in the wake of the Iraq debacle, and this is something that should be borne in mind as one element of the political background to its active efforts to encourage the development of Islamic financial services.

Unfortunately, there are also political dangers in appearing to be too favourably inclined towards the country's two million Muslims, because a significant number of the other fifty-eight million citizens are suspicious of, and hostile towards, any attempt to make changes to law, taxation or regulation that make them more accommodating of Muslim concerns. In some quarters, every clause of a Finance Act that helped to encourage the provision of Islamic financial services was greeted as a deeply sinister attempt to introduce 'Islamic law' into the United Kingdom. This was particularly true of the 2003 removal of the double stamp duty requirement, which received a great deal of media attention because it was the first such change. In later years the novelty wore off and there was less reporting of subsequent amendments. The publication that details the response to the consultation on *sukuk* issuance makes a brief reference to some respondents who felt that it was 'inappropriate for the government to issue *sukuk* or to take any action that could result in the incorporation of Sharia'a law into English law'.[12] Reading between the lines, the consultation seems to have attracted correspondence from some of these hostile citizens. This report clearly states, as one of its conclusions, that 'the issuance of a *sukuk* does not require the incorporation of Sharia'a law into English law'.[13] Such fears are usually the product of a misunderstanding of what *shari'a* is, based on reports from countries where repressive regimes have introduced laws that they claim are religiously inspired. To date, there has been no political opposition in the United Kingdom to the promotion of Islamic finance of a nature or intensity that would have disrupted the government's plans in this area. Elsewhere, notably in France, political hostility to any accommodation of Muslim concerns has been a more serious obstacle to the development of Islamic finance. Nevertheless, there are legitimate questions to be raised about how far legislative and regulatory accommodation of Islamic finance ought to go, and its supporters should not assume that any such questioning is always prompted by pure religious hostility.

The future

The first commercial sukuk issuance in Britain was announced just as this book was going to press in August 2010.[14] A company called International Innovative Technologies (IIT), a maker of industrial machinery based in Gateshead in the northeast of England, raised $10 million from a Dubai-based private equity firm through a *musharaka* structured *sukuk*. In the previous month the large UK travel company Thomas Cook failed in an attempt to raise $50 million from Gulf investors through a *sukuk* issuance.[15] The IIT issuance was received as an indication that the Islamic financial markets were recovering but it is too soon to say if this perception is accurate. The most important question concerning *sukuk* in the United Kingdom is whether the new coalition government will proceed with a sovereign *sukuk* issuance. It might well feel that it would be a pity not to go ahead after so much ground work has been done by its predecessor. There is no reason to think that the new government is any less committed than the old one to the two main aims of *sukuk* issuance: namely, to attract investment from overseas, particularly the Gulf, and to make life easier for British Muslims. The outcome will depend in the end on the decisions taken in relation to the radical restructuring of the public finances that the government believes to be necessary.

Notes

1. HM Treasury, *Government Sterling Sukuk Issuance: A Consultation*, November 2007. All these Treasury reports are still available from www.hm-treasury.gov.uk.

2. HM Treasury, *Government Sterling Sukuk Issuance: A Response to the Consultation*, June 2008.

3. HM Treasury and the Financial Services Authority, *Legislative Framework for the Regulation of Alternative Finance Iinvestment Bonds (Sukuk): Summary of Responses*, October 209.

4. HM Treasury, *The Development of Islamic Finance in the UK: The Government's Perspective*, December 2008.

5. The magazine *New Horizon*, one of the main journals about Islamic banking, has published several articles in recent years hailing an imminent British sovereign *sukuk* issuance. The prospect that a devolved Scotland might also be interested in an issuance generated the memorable headline, '"Tartan sukuk" a possibility?' (July–September 2008).

6. HM Treasury, *Government Sterling Sukuk Issuance*, June 2008, p. 27.

7. *National Savings and Investment (NS&I) Sharia'a Compliant Savings Review*, June 2008.

8. 'Sukuk, their applications and challenges', *New Horizon*, July–September 2009.

9. Amin, Mohammed, 'The new UK tax law on sukuk', *New Horizon*, October–December 2007.

10. 'Sukuk it up', *The Economist*, 17 April 2010.

11. 'Testing the limits of Islamic debt', *The Financial Times*, 19 October 2009; 'Defaults destabilise a reviving market', *The Financial Times*, 8 December 2009.

12. HM Treasury, *Government Sterling Sukuk Issuance*, June 2008, p. 11.

13. HM Treasury, *Government Sterling Sukuk Issuance*, June 2008, p. 12.

14. 'First UK Islamic bond launches', *The Financial Times*, 16 August 2010.

15. 'Thomas Cook fails with $50m sukuk', *The Financial Times*, 12 July 2010.

CHAPTER 9
BUSINESS FINANCE

The provision of business banking services in *shari'a* compliant form has not kept pace with the availability of personal financial services. The large-scale corporate finance sector is mostly concerned with companies based outside the United Kingdom, while the provision of banking services to local companies is mostly aimed at small businesses. To date, there have been very few attempts to provide *halaal* venture capital in the United Kingdom. The one notable example is discussed below.

The Islamic Bank of Britain has a dedicated branch for commercial services, opened at the end of 2007. It is situated in the Alum Rock area of Birmingham, the city in which the IBB's head office is also located. Birmingham has a very large Muslim population and one aspect of this is the presence of a great many small businesses run by Muslim families or individuals. The services available through the commercial office are available from any branch, but in this one they are given a particular promotional emphasis. It is open to the public for only two hours a day and works mainly through personal interviews and consultations.

Business bank accounts

The IBB offers both current and savings accounts for businesses.[1] The business current account offers the full range of usual facilities, that is, chequebook, direct debits and standing orders, cash withdrawal and debit card, as well as foreign currency services. It is presently offering a completely free service for the first eighteen months the account is open, unless the turnover of the business exceeds £1 million, in which case normal charges will apply.

The IBB launched its business services with a savings account targeted at mosques and charities. It can be opened with only £1 and there is no limit to the number of withdrawals that can be made, so it is suitable for organisations that handle only small amounts of money. This is the only one of the bank's accounts that is explicitly described as being suitable for non-Muslims as well, because the bank thinks that non-Muslim charities will be interested in being able to deposit their funds in an account that will use them 'in an ethical and responsible manner'. It uses a *mudaraba* model in the same manner as the personal savings accounts.

There is a straightforward savings account for businesses that can be opened with a minimum of £20 and has no restrictions on withdrawals. It also uses a *mudaraba* structure, that is, it is a profit-and-loss-sharing account. The bank also offers term deposit accounts for businesses, with periods of three, six, twelve, eighteen or twenty-four months. The certificate of endorsement refers to this as using a *mudaraba* principle, whereas the personal term deposit accounts use a *wakala* arrangement. The bank explains that in order to be legitimate there has to be an element of risk with these accounts, but that it 'is employing a number of risk mitigating strategies including a profit stabilisation reserve and investing in stable commodities'. Because of this 'no customer has ever suffered a loss'.

Another IBB account available to businesses is a treasury account with a minimum deposit of £100,000. This uses a *murabaha* contract, where the profit is made by buying and immediately re-selling the same commodities. The IBB also offers a personal treasury account with a minimum deposit of £50,000 that uses a *wakala* contract, with the bank acting as the customer's agent to make a profit on trading. The distinction between business and personal banking is evidently not rigid in this case, as the size of the minimum deposit involved means that it will be suitable for some businesses as well as individuals, and the bank states that this *wakala* treasury account is open to businesses, charities and mosques as well. It is available in euros and US dollars as well as sterling. The business treasury account with the higher minimum deposit makes no mention of being available in other currencies.

The IBB also offers a business finance facility that uses the same commodity trading *murabaha* structure as the personal finance plan. It is available only to 'sole traders, partnerships, charities, masjids and madrasahs', not to limited companies. The minimum finance available is £1,000 and the maximum £20,000, which places it firmly in the small business and self-employed sector. (It seems a little strange that the minimum amount that can be advanced under a personal finance contract is as high as £5,000, while the business finance has a lower minimum.)

The United National Bank does not offer any accounts specifically described as business accounts, but its *mudaraba*-based savings accounts are open to businesses, charities and mosques as well as to individuals. In the communities that it serves there are many small family-run businesses, where personal and business banking are often closely linked. Its in-branch promotional material lays emphasis on its money transfer service for sending remittances to Pakistan. This reminds us that international networks are an important aspect of the British Muslim financial market.

HSBC and Lloyds do not at present offer any Islamic accounts for businesses.

Commercial property

The removal of the requirement to pay stamp duty land tax twice on *ijara* home purchase finance that came into force in 2003 applied only to individuals, as did its extension in 2005 to *musharaka* finance. In 2006, the exemption was extended to the purchase of property using Islamic contracts by corporate entities. This has increased the potential market for home purchase finance to include properties that are business premises rather than homes, and the purchase of properties that are homes but whose owners are companies acquiring rental investments.

It is still not the case though that all the home purchase plans discussed in Chapter 5 can be used to purchase commercial property. HSBC Amanah home purchase finance cannot be used to purchase commercial properties, or even buy-to-let properties. In fact, HSBC's home purchase plan is the most restrictive of all those currently available. (It excludes commercial, buy-to-let and shared ownership properties, as well as anything in Scotland.) The UNB 'Islamic mortgage' can be used to purchase business premises.

The Manzil home purchase finance from Ahli United Bank is available only for residential property. However, both *murabaha* and *ijara* finance can be used for buy-to-let properties, which are in a sense commercial. In fact. the bank encourages its customers to 'build a portfolio of properties', and stresses that its purchase plans are available to companies and trusts.[2] Ahli says explicitly that it recognises that there are few other available forms of *shari'a* compliant investment and that this is the main reason why Muslims may wish to purchase more properties after they have acquired their own home.

In the past British Muslims made disproportionate use of property ownership as a form of investment. This was partly due to the experience of housing insecurity of the first generation of migrants, which led them to attach particular importance to the sense of security derived from owning a tangible piece of property, and partly to a lack of other forms of investment that were felt to be religiously acceptable. One of the case studies on inheritance tax planning reported by the OneE group concerns the case of 'a widow in her 70s' who owned seven properties, presumably accumulated by her family over the years.[3] Investment funds based on property rather than on equities were also popular, as they fulfilled some of the functions of mutual funds in a portfolio in the absence, until recently, of any *shari'a* compliant mutual funds. The fall in the property market in the last few years has prompted many Muslim investors to diversify their portfolios by seeking other forms of compliant investments, but this cultural attachment to property is likely to remain for some time.

The IBB is at present the only bank offering finance specifically designed for the purchase of small-scale commercial property. This is available in England and Wales only (the home purchase finance is also available in Scotland). It uses the same structure of *ijara* combined with diminishing *musharaka* as the home purchase plan. It can be used for equity release and refinancing as well as purchase. Leasehold properties can be considered as long as the lease still has at least twenty-five years to run. The minimum deposit is 30 per cent, which is rather better than the finance to value ratio presently available on the bank's home finance. The repayment period can be as short as one year or anything up to a more usual twenty-five years. The IBB's commercial property finance appears to be aimed mostly at the small business owner wishing to purchase premises for their own business rather than at those seeking to build up a 'portfolio' of commercial property. It was noted earlier that a higher proportion of British Muslims than of the general population are self-employed, and the ability to purchase small business premises in a *halaal* manner was an important unmet need for many until recently. The minimum amount that can be considered is £100,000 and the maximum £2.5 million. It is doubtful whether IBB has funded many purchases at the higher end of this range. It was reported to have financed its first £1 million property purchase in 2006.

Insurance of the property, presumably in a non-compliant form, since this is the only kind presently available, is compulsory, with the choice of the purchaser taking out a policy directly or of paying the bank to do it. The bank also states that the purchaser will be responsible for all repairs to the property, but that there may be cases where their *shari'a* advisers consider that the bank is obliged to refund the cost of certain repairs. In the past scholars usually considered that if the customer who is paying rent for the use of the property is obliged to pay repair costs that cannot be known in advance, this introduces an element of *gharar* into the contract, and therefore took the view that the owner, that is, the bank, should be responsible for them in order to make the contract fully *halaal*. In practice, no bank is keen to take on this responsibility; in fact, it was something which made conventional banks reluctant to begin offering Islamic home purchase finance.

The Bank of London and the Middle East is a specialist in the provision of *shari'a* compliant finance for high-end or large-scale property purchase to companies and high net worth individuals.[4] In addition to providing its own funds to clients, it structures purchases using the funds of external investors. It prides itself on its ingenuity in developing Islamic solutions to challenging property purchase situations. One of its case studies describe how an *ijara* contract could not be used because the bank was not the sole owner of the property involved, and so it devised a 'fixed rate *tawarruq*' structure. The application of a *tawarruq* model (already considered suspect by some scholars) to property purchase is a striking new development. Essentially, the finance for the purchase is provided by trading in metals with the involvement of a broker, like the personal finance facility described in Chapter 4 but on a larger scale. This also has the advantage of avoiding the taxation issues that arise with other property finance contracts.

The BLME's focus is on prestigious areas of London, but its clients do sometimes venture out into other areas of the British property market that look promising. (The *tawarruq* case study concerns a garden centre in Peterborough.) Its most recent property newsletter contains an interesting discussion on the relative merits of the commercial and residential sectors for investment. Traditionally, commercial property has been seen as the most suitable for a long-term investment because tenants commit themselves for longer periods, but the bank's experts report that residential buy-to-let investments actually show a higher return. The BLME wishes to encourage the development of portfolios of corporately managed residential property. As we have seen, property portfolios are something of a theme in British Muslim investment, and it is easy to see how a new generation of Muslim investors could develop tradition into a large-scale corporate model.

The bank reinforces the most recurrent refrain in Islamic finance by displaying in its information material the motto 'real security only ever comes from real assets'.

This expresses very neatly the way that a cultural preference for property ownership which is a characteristic result of the migration experience merges with the religious principle that all finance must be based on tangible assets. Significantly, BLME says that its services include 'advice on recent UK legislation that allows competitive Islamic financing'. A hostile interpretation of the situation might be that the efforts of the UK government to promote equality of treatment for Islamic property purchase contracts has made it easier for companies and wealthy individuals based overseas to buy prime properties in the country.

Gatehouse Bank is primarily a provider of asset management services, but real estate features prominently among the range of assets that it manages, often in the form of property funds.[5] Its property services are not confined to the United Kingdom, but have a 'global remit'. It mentions the securitisation of real estate assets in the form of *sukuk* as one of the services it offers. The possibility of being able to offer this kind of securitisation of property assets in the form of tradable *sukuk* was one development of the Islamic financial markets in the United Kingdom that the government hoped to promote through its own sovereign *sukuk* issuance. At present the City of London is handling these types of assets, but they originate abroad and often the investors who buy them are also based abroad.

Structuring of business finance

The BLME arranges large-scale Islamic financing for companies based in the United Kingdom, the United States and Europe. It specialises in leasing (*ijara*) contracts for equipment. Nearly all the case studies it advertises concern companies based in the United States. This is a prime example of the expertise in Islamic financing arrangements that has been built up in the United Kingdom being employed in the service of clients with no direct connection with the country. The same applies to Gatehouse Bank, which has arranged some large-scale financing contracts for overseas clients. Its most recent news release concerns an *ijara* financing structure secured on Kuwaiti oil rigs, involving several Kuwaiti banks. Stories of this type of commercial activity could be multiplied, but they tell us little about the development of Islamic finance in the United Kingdom as it relates to the British Muslim community.

Venture capital

1st Ethical now has a venture capital operation, which it calls its 'business angel' division.[6] It was a long-held dream of the founders of the company to create an Islamic venture capital fund and they spent several years trying to secure the commitment and financial pledges that would make it possible. They were determined that the project would not proceed until it was on a secure footing, because a botched attempt would tarnish the image of Islamic financing for a long time to come. A minimum figure of £3 million was identified, but by 2006 only £2 million had been promised. Then 'a consortium of business acquaintances' promised another £10 million, and the venture capital fund was secure. The first money was given out in early 2008. The company does not advance its own money, but puts potential investors and businesses that need capital in touch with each other. It does not charge an arrangement fee, but will sometimes take an equity share in the business in lieu of one. It seems that individual members of staff of 1st Ethical, as opposed to the company itself, often invest in the businesses that they help. The impression is that there is a strong element of personal networking involved.

The minimum finance that can be arranged is £100,000 and the maximum £500,000, and this is normally obtained from four or five investors. The company will not handle businesses outside the United Kingdom, 'unethical' businesses or any form of property purchase or development, because one of its aims is to move Islamic finance on from the disproportionate emphasis to date on property purchase. True to the spirit of its tax planning associate, OneE Tax, 1st Ethical has identified an entitlement to tax relief for many of the businesses concerned. The Enterprise Investment Scheme grants exemption from some income and capital gains taxes on the profits made by investors in qualifying small businesses. It also apparently confers an exemption from regulation by the FSA, which is useful since the 'angel' aspect of 1st Ethical is not so regulated.

The Islamic model used is a *musharaka* model, a form of business funding that would be conventionally known as 'equity financing'. Rather than being given a loan that must be repaid regardless of how the company performs, entrepreneurs repay the investment by granting the investors a share in the ownership of the business, which means that the investors share in the profits. This share in the ownership of a company is the origin of the kind of 'shares' traded on the financial markets, but most of that trading activity has lost sight of any connection with the funding of the business. If there are no profits, entrepreneurs are relieved of the pressure of having to repay a debt out of income they do not have created by a conventional loan. The company states forthrightly that the question of whether this type of financing is 'competitive' with a conventional bank loan for the entrepreneur does not arise, because there is no direct comparison between the two modes of financing.

1st Ethical is insistent that this is the true Islamic model of business finance. Some writers on the subject feel strongly that *mudaraba* is the most truly Islamic type of contract. The difference between the two is that in a *musharaka* arrangement losses as well as profits are shared, whereas under a *mudaraba* contract profits are shared but losses are borne solely by the party who has advanced the capital and not by the business manager, who is considered to have lost enough in time and effort. The company's view of this is that expecting investors to stand all losses while the recipient of the funds does not share them is not realistic in the modern world and that it would be difficult to attract investment under such a model.

The company views independent health practitioners, such as dentists, as a promising field of investment and also a safe one, because the rules of their professional associations oblige them to conduct their financial affairs with propriety. Its favourite case study of its venture capital in action also concerns health care. A talented pharmaceuticals researcher had developed and patented a new form of drug delivery that he wished to exploit commercially. As a committed Muslim he did not wish to accept an interest-bearing loan and also believed that the absence of the pressure of having to repay a loan in a fixed time would enable him to concentrate on the long-term growth of the business, known as Nemaura Pharma. An application of his invention to the treatment of diabetes later resulted in a spin-off company known as Dermal Diagnostics, which now claims to be close to having its product licensed for use.

This is an interesting story for several reasons. It establishes that a product with the potential to be a great commercial success can be funded by *shari'a* compliant means. It shows Islamic financing being chosen partly because it is actually better suited to the needs of the entrepreneur and not just because it is a religious obligation. It involves a profession that forms part of the repertoire of stereotypes of British Muslims. The 'Asian' doctor, dentist and pharmacist (and, of course, accountant) are social clichés in Britain, reflecting the preference of immigrants for their children to enter careers that carry a status high enough to outweigh racial prejudice and in which gaining employment is based on unarguable paper qualifications and not on nebulous experience or contacts that will always disadvantage recent arrivals. The transition from pharmacist to owner of a pharmaceuticals company is a bridge from a restricted field of career preference, still influenced by the experience of migration, to an expectation of success in any field of endeavour, and of the right to succeed without compromising cultural and religious belief.

It should, however, be emphasised that other businesses for which 1st Ethical has arranged finance are by no means stereotypical. One recipient is a florist, specialising in weddings. The company uses his story to deliver a lesson in how a business can grow by exploiting specialist knowledge of the 'Asian' market while still catering for the general customer. Another success story is a franchisee of the entirely mainstream Costa Coffee chain, who wished for finance to purchase an additional store in 'the quaint market town of Kettering'. This individual preferred *musharaka* financing even though he had been approved for a conventional bank loan.

1st Ethical reports that there are more investors wishing to put money into companies than there are companies worth investing in. They find that too many proposals submitted to them are excessively idealistic and lack a realistic business plan, while they insist on commercial viability first and foremost. This observation of the prevalence of idealism among those seeking *shari'a* compliant finance forms an interesting counterpart to what is often seen as the cynicism of the large banks that have entered the field.

The future

Representatives of 1st Ethical once took advantage of a visit to their offices by the Governor of the Bank of England to complain about British Asians being particularly badly hit by the threat to the native textile industry, because a disproportionate number of them are or have been involved in the textile industry.[7] With a particularly cruel historical irony, cheaper labour costs in the Indian sub-continent are now driving jobs away from the country to which the first generation of migrants came and towards the countries that they left. This experience moved the company to a plea for protectionism that was never likely to find a response in the present political climate. Fundamentally, however, those British Muslims active in business recognise the need to diversify the types of products and services in which their community is involved.

If it is to be successful and make a permanent contribution to life in the United Kingdom then Islamic finance needs to have an economic base at home. The investment of large amounts of money from overseas sources in Islamic banking in Britain has in its own way been a form of redistribution of wealth, because it has enabled British Muslims to benefit from religiously compliant financial services that would not have been viable on the basis of the home market alone. But the long-term stability of the Islamic financial sector can be ensured only by the existence of thriving Muslim businesses in Britain.

An additional benefit of an Islamic form of financing is that it keeps wealth within the Muslim community. The first generation of migrants to Britain were largely forced to keep their money within their own community because of their lack of understanding of, and acceptance by, the agencies of the wider society. As they became increasingly integrated into British society this economic self sufficiency was weakened. Instead of paying rent to fellow countrymen they began paying back loans from high street banks, or rent and fees to mainstream lettings agencies. The emergence of Islamic financial services offers a means of reducing the outflow of Muslim assets to non-Muslim banks and other businesses and of recycling it to help meet some of the needs of the community. Business financing in a *musharaka* or shared equity form has real potential to redistribute wealth in a meaningful way, and to help to close the gap between the most and the least affluent members of the British Muslim community that has become so alarmingly wide. In the end it may well be business financing that turns out to be the most innovative end of Islamic finance, by doing something genuinely different from conventional finance and not just mimicking it.

It is the opinion of some historians that Islamic financial mechanisms were introduced into Europe via the trading contacts of the Italian city-states with the Arab world.[8] A type of business financing known in Italian as *commenda* was found in medieval Europe. It had the distinctive feature that the entrepreneur himself contributed only his labour to the business, yet shared the profits equally with the investor who had provided the capital. This appears to be identical to a *mudaraba* contract. The fact that some of the European vocabulary of banking is derived from Arabic[9] tends to reinforce the belief that the Arab world transmitted the Muslim endorsement of trade to a Europe still in the grip of the Christian Church's disapproval of it. Perhaps the Muslim communities of Europe could once again inspire the majority society with their heritage of belief in honest trade as a means of improving society, by creating and redistributing prosperity and also by facilitating the exchange of ideas and values.

Notes

1. All the information about business bank accounts and commercial property purchase can be found on the bank's website at www.islamic-bank.com.

2. www.iibu.com/home/almhome.

3. 1st Ethical Newsletter, Winter 2005/Spring 2006.

4. www.blme.com, accessed 14 June 2010. Details of the *tawarruq* model were taken from a personal communication of 22 June 2010 from Natalie Schoon.

5. www.gatehousebank.com, accessed 14 June 2010.

6. The details of the 1st Ethical venture capital fund's activities are taken from the company's website, www.1stethical.com, several of its newsletters and personal communications from Bashir Timol.

7. 1st Ethical Newsletter, Winter 2004/Spring 2005.

8. Heck, G. W. (2006), *Charlemagne, Muhammad and the Arab Roots of Capitalism*, Berlin: De Gruyter.

9. Notably 'cheque', which comes from an Arabic word referring to a written note of a financial transaction and ultimately from the same root as *sukuk*. The English word cipher and the French *chiffre* (number) both derive from the Arabic word for zero, *sifr*, and so imply an Arab influence on the development of bookkeeping.

CONCLUSION

Before and after the recession
The rapid development in Islamic financial services in the United Kingdom took place during the first seven or eight years of the twenty-first century. While the subsequent global crisis in conventional banking brought the reputation of the industry to an all-time low, it has only increased interest in the Islamic financial sector, which has been perceived to be more stable. The tone of many articles written by Islamic bankers during the period of crisis is distinctly self-congratulatory. However, in harsh practical terms the Islamic sector has suffered too. This book has shown that many promising products have been withdrawn from the market in the face of economic recession and intense risk aversion. Periodic setbacks of this kind are inevitable. The real cause for concern is that the recurrent rhetoric about Islamic finance being more secure because it 'does not create money out of nothing' is often unexamined.

There are increasing worries about the scale of the Islamic sector's exposure to a falling property market. Its promoters emphasise constantly that its strength lies in the fact that in Islamic contracts all finance is secured on a real underlying asset, but what if that real asset is losing value? The surge of activity in Islamic finance in the United Kingdom, particularly in the area of home purchase finance, was at least partly due to the assumption that property prices would carry on rising and that any form of finance secured on a house was virtually risk free. In that sense the Islamic sector's analysis of possible future events was not much more sophisticated than that of the conventional mortgage market whose alleged greed and short-sightedness has been so freely denounced by promoters of the Islamic alternatives.

Both scholarly and journalistic commentators on Islamic finance are now beginning to point out the difference between 'asset based' and 'asset backed'. In the past Islamic financial services have often been 'backed' by physical assets whose precise status in relation to the customer is not entirely clear. There are now calls for Islamic finance to be more directly 'based' on a tangible asset on which the customer has a straightforward claim. This matter has become more urgent in the wake of the high profile defaults and near defaults on *sukuk* payment. As discussed in Chapter 8, there is now doubt about whether the investor has a real claim on the underlying asset. So far this has not been definitively tested in court, but if there were ever to be a court ruling that *sukuk* investors did not, in fact, have such a claim, it would seriously compromise the image of Islamic finance as being qualitatively different from conventional finance.

There are also real issues to be clarified regarding the relative positions of bank and customer in the event of default on home purchase plans. To date, the banks have adopted such conservative lending criteria for Islamic home finance that they have been able to avoid any court cases, but if this type of finance is to become a permanent and growing industry it will inevitably encounter some defaults. A test case that established what exactly the formulations about 'joint ownership' and 'sharing risk' mean in hard legal reality is in the long term both unavoidable and desirable.

Some commentators seem to feel that the *sukuk* defaults threaten the whole of the Islamic financial services industry, but this is too sweeping a view. The present recession and the problems in the banking industry, both in the conventional and the Islamic sectors, will eventually pass. In the long run they may be seen not as marking the beginning of the end of Islamic finance, but rather as marking the beginning of a new phase of maturity in the industry, particularly in the United Kingdom. The Islamic financial services industry is being forced to address the issues and weaknesses that have been exposed by the downturn. It will no longer be able to get by with vague assertions about Islamic finance being more stable because it has real assets lying behind it. Although the lack of clarity regarding this matter in relation to *sukuk* was first brought to light overseas, it will probably be in the English courts that a definitive answer is finally arrived at. As noted earlier, many companies based abroad choose England as the legal jurisdiction by which their Islamic contract should be governed, because English courts can investigate the matter with greater transparency and less political interference than the courts in some countries. Furthermore, any British government would want to be satisfied about these matters before proceeding with a government *sukuk* issuance.

Another silver lining to the cloud of the recession is that if the Islamic finance industry is no longer being sustained by the sheer exuberance of financial markets generally, it will need to work harder at addressing real economic needs and attracting new customers. The first Islamic products to appear benefited from a large amount of pent-up demand, and some commentators seem to have been misled into thinking that the remarkable rate of growth in the sector in the first few years of the availability of Islamic products in the United Kingdom could be sustained indefinitely. In fact, the rate of growth has declined and much of the activity now involves different providers competing for the same customers. Long-term growth will require attracting new customers, either by persuading people with no previous concern for whether their financial services were *shari'a* compliant that this is something they ought to care about, or by providing products that can compete with conventional ones on price and general attractiveness. At present, some Islamic providers are still a long way from achieving the latter. For Islamic products to be successful in the long term in the United Kingdom their providers will need to work harder on understanding the whole of the British Muslim market and not just going for the easy target of the very wealthy.

It has been noted that many Islamic financial transactions concerning parties based in other countries, particularly in the Gulf, are arranged by banks and lawyers in the United Kingdom, because of the critical mass of expertise that has now accumulated there. This is a great opportunity for the United Kingdom to build on. The job opportunities thus created may be one answer to the problem of how to transfer some wealth from the oil states to impoverished British Muslims. The fact that most such opportunities will be in London presents its own danger, that this could simply worsen the problem of the internal migration of the most able and ambitious Muslims from other regions of the United Kingdom to the capital, leaving behind communities deprived of their natural leadership who will have to struggle even harder to escape from a cycle of disadvantage. There is still plenty of scope for British Muslim entrepreneurs to build successful businesses of all kinds, including financial services, in their local communities, and with modern communications technology it should surely be possible to create new hubs of Islamic financial expertise in other regions of the country. The OneE group is still headquartered in Bolton, Lancashire, and Parsoli chose Dewsbury, Yorkshire for its main UK office. The devolved Scottish government is known to be interested in promoting financial services as a key industry of the future and would support efforts to build up the Islamic financial sector in Scotland. An Islamic Finance Council was founded in Glasgow in 2005. It helped banks to adapt their home purchase plans to Scottish property law and claims that this is in some ways closer to the spirit of *shari'a* than its English equivalent. Whether overseas companies will be convinced by this claim remains to be seen.

At present there is something of a misalignment between the theoretical research into Islamic economics and the creation of actual marketable products. While a great deal of work goes into the technical design and religious approval of new *shari'a* compliant products, there is often not enough effort put into their presentation to customers, especially in the British context. In the future it will not be enough to simply be Islamic and expect customers to be grateful for this. While admittedly many conventional banks also display standards of customer service that leave something to be desired, Islamic banks still tend to do worse in this regard, and in future Muslim customers whose standard of comparison is the most successful British companies of all kinds will increasingly demand better.

The exclusion of the poor

At present there is a substantial gap between the Islamic finance of the rich and that of the poor. Any visitor to the United Kingdom can see this on a small scale by taking the Metropolitan line of the London Underground from Edgware Road to Whitechapel Road. The IBB has branches in both of these locations. Edgware Road is the centre of the Arab community in London and Whitechapel Road that of the Bangladeshi community in the capital. Naturally, the cultural differences between these two communities are evident in many ways in the shops and restaurants in the two areas. More importantly for a financial study, the banks in Edgware Road indicate a substantial overlap between products aimed at Muslims and products aimed at the wealthy. The local branch of HSBC has a dedicated Amanah service area. It also, at the time the writer visited, had a large and prominent display of the brochure that describes the bank's Premier account, a conventional account available exclusively to those able to pay in at least £100,000 per annum. The Whitechapel branch of HSBC displayed only a few token examples of this brochure. Barclays Bank, which does not offer any Islamic retail products, has taken the trouble to display greetings in Arabic on the doorway of its Edgware Road branch, which suggests that it does not see its lack of *shari'a* compliant products as deterring all Arab customers. There is no sign of any conventional banks in Whitechapel thinking it worth their while to put up welcoming signs in Bengali.

The IBB also offers a Premier service, and states in its information material that all the staff of the Premier department speak fluent Arabic, which makes clear where they expect their most affluent customers to come from. While it is, of course, not the case that all Arabic speakers are rich, the division between rich and poor among the customers of Islamic banking in the United Kingdom does show a substantial degree of alignment with differences in national and ethnic origin, and there is a danger that resentment of the banks' cultivation of expatriate Arabs by local South Asian Muslims could affect the further development of the Islamic financial sector in the United Kingdom. A more positive interpretation of the situation would be that British Muslims benefit from the inflow of expatriate money, because the British Muslim community alone could not sustain the level of Islamic banking activity now seen in the country.

There is a less obvious, but ultimately more worrying,

division between rich and poor among the permanent Muslim population of the United Kingdom. Compared with the general population, there is only a small middle class among Muslims and larger groups at both extremes of the income scale, those who have done very well in business and those who are struggling to survive on state benefits. This is an obstacle to the growth of Islamic financial services, because it is middle income families who are the main market for conventional financial services, and providers are used to tailoring products for this income level. To date, there has been little serious analysis of how this situation affects demand for *shari'a* compliant products. In fact, there has been little serious study of demand at all. This omission may mean that in the long run the real growth in Islamic finance in the United Kingdom comes not from the giant international banks who were the first to enter the field, and the first to begin to withdraw when the economic climate began to look less promising, but from indigenous companies who have an inside knowledge of the British Muslim market.

The most painful aspect of the present state of the industry is that the poorest Muslim communities may face not only social and economic exclusion, but a form of religious exclusion, if they continue to face a situation where Islamic products are more difficult to access and more expensive than conventional ones. Some observers believe that there is a market for microfinance in the United Kingdom, along the lines of the initiatives developed in Bangladesh, involving the provision of very small amounts of money that can make a disproportionate improvement to the lives of the very poor. (The best known example of this is the work of Grameen Bank, although this operates within a conventional and not an Islamic framework.) An Islamic form of microfinance scheme in British cities could be an exciting development. Something needs to be done to remove the impression sometimes given that Islamic finance is a way for the rich to buy their way into paradise.

Consumerism versus citizenship

There is an ambiguity to the government's promotion of Islamic finance that is rarely explored in sufficient depth. One hostile view of the emergence of the Islamic banking industry internationally is that it is a way of incorporating the Muslim world into the globalised economy, of removing any last awkward points of cultural resistance to the complete globalisation of finance by presenting it in a religiously tailored guise. Whether or not this is true internationally, one interpretation of the British government's eagerness to create the celebrated 'level playing field' for Islamic financial services in the United Kingdom is certainly that it wishes to remove any reason for resistance by British Muslims to complete social, economic and political integration. By making religiously acceptable alternatives to conventional finance available within a framework of control and regulation by government authorised bodies, the emergence of radically oppositional versions of Islamic practice can be contained. Over the last decade successive governments have been anxious to prevent the growth of 'extremist' versions of Islam, and in the field of economics the conclusion that Islamic principles necessitate the end of capitalism, a conclusion sometimes drawn in the more excitable writing on the subject, probably constitutes a form of extremism that makes governments nervous.

One of the most interesting features of Islamic economic thinking is that it cannot be fitted easily into the conventional political divisions of left, or socialist, and right, the advocacy of the pure free market. It is opposed to state socialism and highly positive about business, seeing trade and entrepreneurship as the main means of creating and distributing wealth. On the other hand, it is centrally concerned to prevent the ever increasing accumulation of wealth in the hands of individuals and to keep it constantly flowing around society. This is why it imposes the annual deduction from wealth for charitable purposes, *zakat*. Perhaps one reason why the Labour government that came to power in 1997 with a manifesto commitment to being a 'third way' between socialism and unfettered capitalism was sympathetic to Islamic economics is that it saw in it a related kind of 'third way'. That does not mean necessarily that subsequent governments of other parties will be less sympathetic, because the commitment to managed and regulated capitalism has now become the common ground of British politics, and the management and regulation of capitalism is essentially also what modern Islamic economics is about.

A tension arises when this kind of sympathetic support from government turns into a belief in integration through consumerism rather than through a more explicitly theorised citizenship. In our consumer society the logic of marketing, the power of the brand, runs counter to the political imperative to treat everyone the same, because the marketing need is to maintain the distinctiveness of the product.[1] In advertising terms multiculturalism is expressed as a variety of niche markets. In the long term governments are unlikely to be able to contain the varieties of distinctiveness and opposition that will emerge through the exploration of Islamic economic principles.

Islamic finance as ethical finance

At the rhetorical level Islamic finance is routinely identified with ethical finance. This identification is, in fact, taken virtually for granted by its practitioners and almost never seriously questioned. For someone with a religious faith it is difficult not to believe that their faith defines what is ethical, while for providers there is a strong business incentive to increase their customer base by promoting Islamic services in the wider ethical sector of the market rather than limiting it to Muslims. In practice, there are a number of problems with the attempt to position 'Islamic' as a sub-set of 'ethical'.

At the most fundamental level there is a philosophical difference in the derivation of the standards by which customers regulate their economic behaviour. A secular consumer who identifies their consumption as 'ethical' has made a conscious decision to choose certain products because they conform to a set of values in accordance with which they have elected to live their life. In fact, these values and standards may vary substantially between consumers who all see themselves as 'ethical'. This is quite different from observing a set of prescriptions and proscriptions simply because they have Quranic or Prophetic authority, a form of authority which by definition cannot be questioned. The secular ethical consumer often perceives their behaviour to be a form of rebellion against that prevailing in society as a whole, and using their own judgement about what they think is right rather than being told what to do by an external authority is an important part of their self-definition as ethical. Although the non-Muslim ethical consumer may have respect for religious faith in general, the practical reality that Islamic financial service providers are dependent on the approval of a handful of very powerful and very well paid scholars is seriously at odds with this attitude.

A related point concerns what is known in advertising terminology as 'dilution of the brand'. Muslims who prefer Islamic financial services do so as a rule because they are Islamic, not because they are ethical in some vaguely defined sense. Being strongly branded as Islamic is an important part of their appeal. There is a certain air of exclusiveness about Islamic products, not in the sense that non-Muslims are actually unwelcome as customers, but in as much as choosing an Islamic product over a conventional alternative makes a powerful statement of identification with a certain heritage and of membership in a certain group. To extend the brand by emphasising that a product is ethical rather than that it is *shari'a* compliant will weaken this sense of identification and loyalty, possibly to the point where it will no longer be strong enough to outweigh higher prices or less advantageous terms.

There may be more potential in targeting members of other religious groups. The last few years have seen the appearance of Christian and Jewish investment funds, in some cases directly inspired by the Islamic example.[2] There is broad agreement among the three faiths over which areas are unacceptable for investment, and at least a general openness among Christians and Jews to the idea that interest-based financing is undesirable, since both faiths forbade interest among their own communities in the past.[3] Branding a product in some way as 'Abrahamic', that is, adopting the increasingly popular term 'the Abrahamic faiths', would not threaten Muslim identification with it as much as associating it with secular ethical ideas. However, the fact that many Muslims seek to boycott goods made in Israel could be a serious obstacle to a joint investment enterprise with Jews. More generally, it is entirely possible that having financial services clearly and uniquely identified as an expression of their own faith is just as important to Christians and Jews as to Muslims. As for other religious traditions such as Hinduism, while some writers claim that they also have traditions of hostility to interest payments, there is too much divergence of opinion on which goods are prohibited and too great a legacy of political hostility for a joint approach to have much hope of success.

There are some particular points of likely tension between Islamic and ethical investment criteria. A consensus seems to have emerged over the exclusion of alcohol, tobacco, arms, gambling and pornography from both types of fund. The non-Muslim investor is likely to balk at the blanket exclusion of all forms of media that is adopted by some Islamic funds, particularly as this seems at present to be a promising field for future growth. While the exclusion of pork is an essential part of Islamic investment, the non-Muslim ethical investor is much more likely to have a broad concern for animal welfare that extends (rightly or wrongly) to being unhappy about *halaal* slaughter, and a dual marketed fund would probably have to exclude all animal products. A large percentage of consumers who identify themselves as ethical also identify themselves as feminist, and might, for example, have reservations about investing in the thriving area of 'modest dress' manufacture.

The most glaring reason for a conflict between Islamic and ethical branding is that environmental concerns figure very prominently in the concerns of the self-defined ethical investor. National Savings and Investment concluded that an association with renewable energy was the most promising way of promoting a savings account as both Islamic and ethical. The trouble is that such concerns usually involve a deep hostility to oil companies, and at the present time the wealth of the Arab oil states is the motor driving the whole of the international Islamic finance industry. It would be impossible for any Islamic investment fund to exclude oil companies, whereas some ethical funds with a strong 'green' bias do exclude them. A consumer who sought earnestly to avoid profits derived from oil could not even open an account with IBB.

There is though reason for hope that in the future the oil industry may become a less divisive factor in the related work of Islamic and ethical financial services. All the oil states are now conscious that diversification of their economic base is essential, and investment in renewable energy is a growing aspect of that. The oil companies themselves are acutely aware of the need to make their activities less environmentally damaging, and the disastrous leak from a BP well in 2010 will make their attempts to do so more urgent. Environmentally concerned and Islamic investors could make common cause in pushing companies and states further in this desirable direction. This is the stance adopted by the Friends Provident Stewardship fund, one of the best known 'ethical' funds, which does not automatically exclude oil and gas companies but will invest only in those that are committed to 'reducing their carbon footprint'. The other exclusions adopted by this fund appear identical to those of Islamic funds.[4] It also exercises positive choice of sectors that help to supply basic human needs, which is something many Muslim writers believe should be done but with which much Islamic banking does not in practice concern itself.

Of course, the inclusion of interest-based banking will always make any conventional financial activity, no matter how 'ethical' it may be in other ways, unacceptable to Muslims and therefore unsuitable for dual marketing. Even here though there may be scope for shared involvement in financial services that are of real benefit to the economically disadvantaged. Some of the Islamic financial services studied in this book lack any wider social agenda beyond the narrow aim of being technically *shari'a* compliant. This is particularly true of home purchase finance, which in its present form makes no contribution at all to improving the housing situation of the poor. The pressures of competing with the conventional sector and of satisfying customers who are not in practice willing to accept any real risk of loss are driving 'shari'a technicians' to devise products that differ from conventional ones only in the most formal sense, and that continue the business of making the rich even richer and the poor even poorer that the prohibition of *riba* is supposed to prevent. In future, the real convergence may be between the aspirations to the redistribution of wealth of the wider ethical finance movement and a new kind of Islamic finance which seeks to explore the deeper meanings of *riba*. This would leave the narrow, legalistic kind of Islamic finance that is dominant at the present time to become a largely separate sphere, one that would probably be obliged to concentrate ever more on the expatriate market and would be in danger of becoming increasingly remote from the everyday concerns of British Muslims.

The role of scholars

Probably the single most important factor that will determine the future direction of Islamic financial services in the United Kingdom is the development of the *shari'a* advisory committees. The shortage of scholars with the necessary combination of religious and financial knowledge is often lamented. At present the same half dozen names recur repeatedly on the advisory committees, and this must raise concerns over the effectiveness of the committees' oversight, both because of their excessive workload and because of the lack of a fresh perspective. The shortage of suitably qualified scholars delays the introduction of new products. (One banker was quoted as saying that having the number of a prominent scholar stored in his mobile phone was 'a real competitive advantage'.[5]) It also gives enormous influence to a few individuals, in a way that is arguably unprecedented in the history of Islam. The banking industry has said repeatedly that centralised, globalised standards of *shari'a* compliance are necessary to make the introduction of new Islamic products quicker and easier. It wants internationally accepted reference guides to what is and is not acceptable. Such standardisation risks institutionalising the opinions of certain scholars at a certain time as the last word on the subject. It is understandable that those whose business depends on the continued acceptability of products they have invested a great deal in developing become frustrated by the constant threat of this being challenged. It seems unlikely though that any form of finance, or any other kind of product for that matter, which is based on religious criteria will ever be able to command universal and unquestioning support. It is not in the nature of religious belief that it should. The appearance of complete consensus within the established industry might in fact only encourage the emergence of dissenting views outside it. The tendency of the banks to urge their customers to rely on the endorsement of a familiar scholarly name rather than to exercise their own judgement is partly an attempt to impose *de facto* standardisation, but even if the bankers manage to prevent the appearance of critical statements by the scholars, they will never be able to control the opinions of their customers.

There is a sense of aversion to *shari'a* risk as much as to the usual forms of financial risk. Relying on the same scholars as all the other banks means that if (to take the most prominent example) Nizam Yaquby's endorsements of a particular bank's products are ever subjected to attack by other schools of scholarship, then at least all its competitors will be going down with it. The result is a kind of 'group think' that stifles real debate. There should be a role for dissent and creativity in thinking about the social role that Islamic finance should play and the technical means it uses to achieve that. Perhaps a new generation of scholars will be able to perform this role, and perhaps some of them could be from Britain. Apart from anything else, looking at the issue of religious approval purely from a business perspective, if the supply of suitably qualified scholars increases then their price, that is their fees, will fall, and that would go some way to making Islamic products more competitive with conventional ones. For this reason the development of the Al-Qalam panel of British scholars has far-reaching implications. If approval from them becomes a reliable low cost alternative to that of expensive scholars based in the Middle East, this will make the introduction of Islamic products in the United Kingdom easier and will also allow them to become more carefully tailored to the UK market. It may be though that the marketing power of established 'brand name' scholars is felt to confer such an advantage that the major banks will be reluctant to part with them. Once again, a bold break with established practice is more likely to come from a company with a real base in the British Muslim community than from an international bank.

To date, much of the development of the Islamic finance industry has been supply led. Providers have, therefore, needed to stimulate demand from those Muslims who are not so far unequivocally demanding Islamic options, and this has led to a blurring of the distinction between education and marketing. After reading a large volume of publicity material about Islamic financial services it becomes evident that it is not the case that British Muslims know exactly how Islamic home finance, for example, works and just need to find someone who supplies it. On the whole, they need to be told how *ijara*, *musharaka* and *murabaha* work. All the banks devote a large part of the information they supply to potential customers to explaining how the Islamic contracts are structured, why they are *shari'a* compliant and why Muslims ought, therefore, to prefer them to the non-compliant alternatives. There is an obvious conflict of interest between the educational and the marketing functions of such material, and so far the secular regulatory bodies seem to have done more to point this out than the scholars.

The well-known author Tariq Ramadan has adopted the optimistic position that Muslims in Europe will play a key role in the future development of Islam, because they are able to engage in religious scholarship and activity free from the twin pressures of crushing poverty and political repression that afflict too much of the Muslim-majority world.[6] In the field of finance at least this interpretation seems very plausible.

Relevance to theories of human behaviour

Some members of the general public express astonishment that religious belief should 'still' influence behaviour in a field usually perceived as entirely secular, that of financial services. There is a popular belief that the activities of the City of London are the last word in modernity, while the traditions of Islam are 'medieval'. At a more academic level the growth of Islamic finance challenges what is known as secularisation theory, which was the dominant view among writers on religious studies for most of the twentieth century. This argued that primitive societies engaged in magic, more developed societies practised a less irrational kind of religion, and that in the highly industrialised societies of the modern world religion would eventually disappear altogether. There is, indeed, some correlation between high levels of economic development and low levels of formal religiosity, but there is also evidence that affluence produces an increase in concern for social justice, and this often has a religious expression. A recent study[7] produced empirical evidence that concern for the fair distribution of goods increases with a society's degree of integration into the market economy and therefore remoteness from subsistence agriculture. This is somewhat counter-intuitive for anyone brought up in the Christian tradition that disparages trade as morally suspect, but presents no difficulty for someone familiar with the centrality of the moralised market economy in Islam, a tradition in which trade provides both examples and metaphors for the godly life.

Consumer movements demanding that goods are produced in ways that are 'ethical' or that constitute 'fair trade' are seen only in what are known as 'post-scarcity societies', that is, those where mere physical survival is taken for granted and most people can afford the bare necessities of life with only a small proportion of their income. In these circumstances people want their spending to provide something more than the basic pleasure of owning the goods, they seek some kind of deeper satisfaction from the consciousness that their consumption is doing good for others or that it has some kind of spiritual dimension. Islamic finance can be seen in one sense, therefore, as a post-scarcity consumer movement. The first Muslim migrants to the United Kingdom usually left villages that had a basic survival culture, but their grandchildren are growing up in an affluent developed economy. From this perspective it is not surprising that interest in religiously compliant financial services is growing in modern Britain.

Notes

1. Evidence for the growing power of the Islamic 'brand' comes from the announcement of a conference scheduled to take place at the Said Business School, Oxford in July 2010. The School describes it as the 'inaugural global Islamic branding and marketing forum' and claims that the international market for *shari'a* compliant goods and services is worth US$2 trillion per annum. The basis of this calculation must

be very questionable, but the fact that companies believe the market to be a growing one is indisputable.

2. 'Vatican-backed ethical index given baptism', *The Financial Times*, 26 April 2010; 'Israelis savour rise in kosher investments', *The Financial Times*, 2 March 2010.

3. Wilson, Rodney (1996), *Economics, Ethics and Religion: Jewish, Christian and Muslim Economic Thought*, London: Palgrave Macmillan.

4. 'Stewardship Criteria and Policies', available at www.friends provident.co.uk.

5. 'Savings and souls', *The Economist*, 6 September 2008.

6. Ramadan, Tariq (1998), *To be a European Muslim*, Leicester: The Islamic Foundation; (2003), *Western Muslims and the Future of Islam*, Oxford: Oxford University Press.

7. Heinrich, Joseph *et al.*, 'Markets, religion, community size and the evolution of fairness and punishment', published in *Science*, 19 March 2010 and reported in *The Economist*, 20 March 2010.

GLOSSARY AND ABBREVIATIONS

Glossary

The terminology of Islamic finance

Though a strict transliteration system from Arabic to English is available, it is not often used outside the academic world, and the English spellings of Arabic terminology used within the financial services industry can and do vary. This glossary shows only the versions used in this book. It is also worth noting that the commonly used English translations of some Arabic terms can at times obscure the subtlety of the underlying concepts and the extent of debate about their interpretation in practice.

alhamdollillah   'praise be to God', an expression of thankfulness

bay' al-'inah   a combination of contracts for deferred sale and immediate purchase of the same goods where the difference in price effectively constitutes a loan to the client

bay' salam   a form of sale with advance payment for future delivery

dar al-harb   literally 'the house of war', the parts of the world where followers of Islam are absent or in a small minority

dar al-Islam   literally 'the house of Islam', the parts of the world where Muslims are in the majority

darura   the principle that necessity can make permissible actions normally forbidden

Eid	usually refers to *Eid al-Fitr*, the festival which marks the end of the fasting month of Ramadan
fatwa	a formal opinion issued by a scholar of Islamic thought
fiqh	the Islamic legal tradition, the body of thought and precedents to which reference is made when decisions on new matters are required
gharar	sometimes translated as 'speculation' but also covers a wide range of contractual uncertainties; one of the main prohibitions in Islamic economic thought
hadith	an account of an action or statement of Prophet Muhammad observed by a contemporary and transmitted through an unbroken chain of record; the *ahadith* (plural) form a source of Islamic principles supplementary to the Quran
haja	need, a weaker form of *darura*
halaal	'permitted', in accordance with Islamic teaching
haraam	'forbidden', unacceptable in Islam
ijara	a form of leasing contract, the most popular model of Islamic home purchase finance
'illa	the essential attribute of a matter which determines which legal principles apply to it, usually translated as 'efficient cause'
imam	one who leads prayers, a Muslim religious leader
jahiliyya	the pre-Islamic period in Arabia
kafala	safekeeping or guardianship, a principle invoked as the basis for several forms of financial service

kameti	a kind of savings club common among Pakistani immigrants to Britain
khutba	'sermon', the address given at Friday prayers in a mosque
madrasah	a school which teaches the religion, law and philosophy of Islam
masjid	a mosque
maslaha	the general welfare of society, the public good
maysir	gambling, games of chance
mudaraba	a form of business finance where one party supplies the capital and the other the labour or entrepreneurial initiative and profits are shared in agreed proportions
mudarib	the person who does the work, the entrepreneur, in a *mudaraba* arrangement
murabaha	a combination of contracts for purchase and immediate re-sale at a higher price, a common form of Islamic home purchase finance
musharaka	a form of business finance where two or more parties contribute capital to a venture and share the profits in agreed proportions
nisab	the threshold of wealth above which one becomes liable to *zakat*
qard	a loan
qard hasan	literally a 'good loan', a loan where only the principal is repaid, without any addition
qiyas	the principle of analogy, one of the ways in which legal decisions concerning new situations are derived from existing precedents
rab al-maal	literally 'the master of the money', the person who supplies the capital in a *mudaraba* contract

riba	an unacceptable form of increase of capital, usually identified with bank interest; the most important prohibition in Islamic economic thought
sadaqa	any form of voluntary charitable giving, distinct from *zakat*
sakk	a document proving entitlement to the proceeds of an asset; it is the singular of *sukuk* but this singular form is rarely seen in English language material
shari'a	literally the 'path' of Islam, the entire body of principles which constitutes the religion of Islam; often translated as 'Islamic law' but it is not comparable to a secular legal code
sukuk	a form of financial instrument which serves a similar function to bonds and bills in conventional finance; the word is the plural form of *sakk* but is often used in English as if it were a singular noun
Sunna	the example of the life of Prophet Muhammad as a guide to correct behaviour
sura	a chapter of the Quran
tabarru	donations, the contributions paid by members of a *takaful* scheme
takaful	'mutual assurance', an Islamic form of insurance
tawarruq	a combination of contracts for deferred sale and immediate purchase of the same goods where the difference in price effectively constitutes a loan to the client, sometimes considered to be identical with *bay' al-inah*
wakala	agency
wakeel	agent

waqf	a gift of property in perpetuity to a charitable cause
zakat	the 2.5% of one's wealth above a certain threshold (*nisab*) which must be donated to charity annually

Abbreviations

AAOIFI	Accounting and Auditing Organisation for Islamic Financial Institutions
ABC	Arab Banking Corporation
BCCI	Bank of Credit and Commerce International
BLME	Bank of London and the Middle East
CTF	Child Trust Fund
EIIB	European Islamic Investment Bank
FSA	Financial Services Authority
HBOS	Halifax Bank of Scotland
HMRC	Her Majesty's Revenue and Customs, the United Kingdom taxation authority
HPP	Home Purchase Plan, the general name given by the FSA to Islamic forms of home purchase finance
LIBOR	London Inter Bank Offer Rate of interest
NS&I	National Savings and Investment
OIC	Organisation of the Islamic Conference
RPI	Retail Prices Index, a measure of inflation
SPV	Special Purpose Vehicle, part of the structure of *sukuk*
SWIP	Scottish Widows Investment Partnership
UNB	United National Bank
VAT	Value Added Tax, the main United Kingdom purchase tax

INDEX